SONGS FOR THE DEAD

Poems, 2016—2023

Adam Neikirk

CONTENTS

Title Page
Songs for the Dead
Preface
I: Songs for the Dead   1
Quitting Cam For Ever [1793]   3
Three Sonnets on the Wind   5
The Shore   7
1630   9
The Religious Personality   11
Apollo   12
The Lonely Tower   13
The Wretch   16
To Albion   17
Pastoral Sonnet   18
The Forlorn Flower   19
Lines on the Platonic Philosophy   20
On the Symposium of Plato   21
Translation of the Soul   22
To Coleridge   23
Natal Sonnet   24
Devotion   25

The Conjurer	27
On the 250th Birthday of William Wordsworth	29
The Treasury of Love	30
The Creation Mix	32
The Necromancer and William Wordsworth	34
Love Ages	36
A Silent Film	37
II: More Songs	39
A Description of Poetry	40
A Poor Man's Fantasy	41
Climbing The Hill	43
Constancy to an Ideal Objector	44
Do Sith Dream of Elected Sheep?	46
Dreams	48
Exemplar	50
Four Forms of Love	51
How do Dreams become Reality?	53
Three Beginnings	55
Laura	56
Mirri's Lament	57
Mushrooms of Westfield	58
Mystical Love	60
Noctilucence	62
Nowhereville	64
Of Styx and Lily Pads (Mono no Aware)	65
On Wordsworth's "Immortality" Ode	67

One Whom Times Elide (For S.T.C.)	71
Returning to Hammersmith on Foot	73
Reverence of the Invisible	75
Scafell	78
Scene of the Crime	81
Self-Love	83
The Blue Shirt	85
The Fading Storm	87
The Hook	89
The Old Millennial	90
The Sea of Sadness	92
The Sparrow and the Cardinal	93
The Spoon	96
"The Two Sisters"	97
There Is No Light	99
Unending Winter	100
To Be A Tree	102
World of Diamonds	104
III: Colchester	107
A Letter to Stoney, composed 27 November 2019	108
A river rippling over the sand	115
Asrael	117
Christmas Season, 1817; or "The Time Machine"	120
For R. W. (1967 – 2009)	125
Hartley's Expostulation / Derwent's Reply	127
How Many Drops?	129

Mister Esteesi	130
Notebook Speculations	131
On 'The Bondage of Love'	132
Poetical Autobiography	134
Solitude	135
Stylish Doom	137
Symposium	138
The Dead	140
The Expert	141
The Hedge Witch	143
The Last Days of a Magician [fragment]	144
The Spirit of Reason	147
Through the Layers of Foundation & the Beauty-Mark	149
To My Students	151
"Undoubtedly"	153
Utopia	155
Your Little Heart	159
IV: Ipswich	163
Anima	164
Aright	165
Celebrating my Ph.D. as a Diabetic	166
Celeste	167
Death and Taxidermy	169
Eating Dessert	170
Ghostly Grove	172

Grief	173
I love to watch your sleeping face	174
In England	175
Job	177
Laying Under the Christmas Tree	178
Luigi	180
Milkweed	182
Nyang	184
Old Bluebell	186
Please Can You Remove Me from This Mailing List	187
Prologue	189
Puffy Hat	191
Ramona	193
Suddenly	196
Take My Car	198
Teen Gohan	199
The Clown	201
The God of Games	203
The Headsman's Axe	205
The Idea of Writing	207
The Imagination	211
There's No Place	213
Thou'rt Still Cool	215
Title	216
To be read as if ...	217
Vast Compass	219

Waiting Room of the Damned	221
Your Valley Life is a Fantasy Life	223
About The Author	225
Books By This Author	227

SONGS FOR THE DEAD

POEMS, 2016–2023

*for my grandfather,
H.R. Stoneback*

Adam Neikirk

Copyright © 2023 by Adam Neikirk. All rights reserved. *Songs for the Dead* was published in 2016 by Des Hymnagistes Press in West Park, NY, USA. ISBN 978-0-99-73461-3-8.

PREFACE

Songs for the Dead was originally published in 2016 by Des Hymnagistes Press. This was my grandfather's press and he helped me to gather up and edit what I thought of as my best poems and to form them into a book. At the time, I was virtually unknown as a poet and my grandfather's choice to help me publish was purely to encourage me to pursue a literary career, rather than gain anything monetarily. That said, Des Hymnagistes Press was his personal press, and I think he largely used it to self-publish his own books of poetry. He would then use his connections as a writer and academic to do poetry readings where he would sell his books. I suppose this made a bit of economic sense, and also allowed him to publish at a much greater rate. His name was H.R. Stoneback, a poet, songwriter, and modernist specializing in Hemingway and Faulkner studies.

My grandfather died in December of 2021, in bed in his large home in Highland, NY, where he had lived alone for the last several years. At the time of his death I was living in the United Kingdom with my partner (and later wife) Sheryl. I didn't know that he was in poor health, if he was, and his death happened suddenly and silently from afar, which made it feel surreal to me. Some of his surviving family suspect that he died from complications due to COVID-19. However, no autopsy was performed, and so the cause of his death remains a mystery.

These two facts partly explain my choice to self-publish this expanded and revised volume of poems, which includes the original *Songs for the Dead*'s 24 poems (unchanged from the original) as well as a selection of unpublished poems from 2017 to 2023, which I have curated and which brings the total to 110. Now that my grandfather has passed on, I do not think Des Hymnagistes will be a functioning press any longer, and furthermore, I want to give myself a good reason to go back and revisit some of my writing from the last several years. I also want to try self-publishing, which I have never done before.

I should also point out another factor in my decision to self-publish: I am disillusioned with the current publishing landscape that is available to contemporary poets. In my experience, there is a strange and almost parasitical relationship between the many small, independent, sometimes online-only presses that exist, and the kind of poetry that is being written and published around the world. Much of this poetry feels "written to be published" but does not seem to want to engage, either a reading public that is not initiated into the world of professional poets and poetry publishing, or else a poetic tradition that goes back further than the last fifty or one hundred years. Many presses actively discourage "poetical" submissions (for all the sense that makes) and seek to expand or subvert the idea of poetic form by publishing experimental work. On the other hand, there are few, if any, presses that want to publish poems that deal with contemporary subject matter through techniques of versification, and/or those that put the authors in dialogue with historical verse cultures (still actively studied by academics but largely absent from the contemporary poetic landscape). In fact, I feel that there is a kind of hostile silence in the treatment of submitted work that purports to be "verse" (rather than the much harder to define "poetry"), i.e., writing that uses and embraces lineation through physical-linguistic tropes such as rhyme and meter. Yet, for my own part, I see "verse" as a practice and outcome that creates the impetus for writing poetry; and I think a shared understanding of versification is the cornerstone of a viable poetical criticism and reading culture.

This means that, essentially, to own and curate a press or journal is to control the very idea of poetry as a medium for human thought and feeling, as well as to moderate the kind and amount of criticism that can be successfully performed by professional academics and the general reading public. One is also relatively insulated from having to air the fact of this cultural power to others. Many poets whose work is rejected from contemporary presses (and journals) do not receive any indication that they have been denied publication due to cultural or curatorial reasons, and for the most part the decision-making processes behind acceptances and rejections to poetry journals remain opaque. The only thing we experience, as general readers who witness the birthings of new poems in presses and as books, are the results of these secret processes. Thus, good poetry is good because the right people say it is, and bad poetry is never exposed to critique at all because it will presumably never be published. Unfortunately, we can never have a conversation about what it means to express oneself successfully, or even what counts as "good" and "bad" poetry if we behold a functional publishing landscape for poetry that never produces anything that it itself finds objectionable, or, similarly, that frequently produces work that seems to have little in common with the poetical models of the past.

I have tried to finish any poems collected here that I found in an incomplete state. This usually meant adding lines to the poem to round off the form, although doing this also sometimes necessitated making alterations or additions to previous parts of the poem. There were some poems that I liked quite a bit, but that I left out of the collection because they were fragments and I couldn't bring myself to complete them for one reason or another. There are also some long poems that were included in fragmentary form, or which are now divided into several smaller interconnected works (especially in Part IV). These represent attempts at book-length works that simply didn't pan out at the time; I have salvaged any writing from these projects that to me felt capable of standing on its own.

A content warning: some of these poems were written as antidotes to depression and feelings of suicidal ideation, and so the reader should be mindful that, while many poems gathered here express beauty as well as hope and love, some also express aspects of darkness, feelings of emptiness, dejection, woe, and angst. This is nothing new in the poetry world, and I have since (I feel) moved on from the kind of spells that would visit me to produce poems of this latter sort. Yet it is worth mentioning that some like these are here, because I thought they were strong enough to be included.

Finally, in publishing this book through Kindle Create, I hope to use the ubiquity of Amazon's online marketplace to sell digital copies to more people than it would ever reach if it were brought out in a physical form. The original *Songs for the Dead*, which has been in print for seven years now, had a limited run of 150 copies and of those has sold perhaps one third. I often debate with myself if it even makes sense to charge money for poetry, but this way I can at least pursue a more sustainable path of proferring digital poetry that occupies no physical space.

I encourage readers to leave reviews on Amazon's Kindle store, whether or not you like the poetry found here. If you like it, please say so and please direct others to buy and read it. If you don't like it, I would still like to hear your thoughts.

Adam Neikirk
Ipswich, UK & Westfield, MA
2023

I: SONGS FOR THE DEAD

2016

QUITTING CAM FOR EVER [1793]

Early in the year of life,
The birds, the birdsong, the sky and its song
Specific as the scatter of moistened air
Do call to me,
A Riot at my Heart, which feels, and flees—

To leave behind what was given there,
To leave it all and go, anyway,
Away from London, and the center of vice,
From the office and the pulpit now withdraw,
And seek to build true Paradise
On Earth, with my own hand.

A dim flicker in childhood was all
I knew of the magnificent mystery
Which illumines the secret places we keep
Clutched beside us through our life's trial;
Of the ocean-bottom, which dimly light returns
By light refracted, that the surface turns
Upon it; as one wearying discerns
That Pain will beget Providence in Time:
So smiling rests, and shoulders no thought
Of penitence, or releases from its grip.

Early in the year of life,
The birds and the sky were all a piece,
And you could name a single bird as it flew
Across the width of light that makes to view
It catch a single raindrop on its beak—

Nor did we see the sky as dangerous,
We lonely few, Romantic through and through;
Nor found in its resistance to our grasp
A sign of death; nor made of its vastness
The impetus of terror, which cries out!
Out of the heart of the birdsong,
Terror machine of the world.

THREE SONNETS ON THE WIND

The fire of time relays an ashen tale;
The power of story contains the raging fire;
To wander before the fire asks to pain
Luck's wing bent thin and hapless on the gale.
And so the wrist should bend to catch what's fair—
Hold quickly out thy hand, fortunate thief!
A paper dragonfly, or Sibylline;
A ribbon white, to calm the wild hair:
Canst thou read the puny script from where it lies
Unfolded, as thy hair sports in the breeze?
Upon the leaf, the ancient names of things
(Writ like the stained-glass wings of dragonflies)
And other things beside, lay glittering;
Awhile the wood is burning all alive.

O sister! Brother! Friend! Be your fond seat
Ever it is; mayst thou find it, stopping here.
The sorrowful ribbon, yet to no one dear,
Unfolded, shivers on thy folded knees,
An orphan, fleeing time on the giving wind!
The voice, its small sound but a current lone,
One shivering in multitude, hath grown
More desperate, in a jabbing, restless hand
Composed; to list, and yield a whisper soft,
Saddened, perhaps, with distance, but not lost
To melancholy—not yet! Only read,
With thine eyes, thy mind, and thy heart aloft
A glow of universal sympathy
(Uncanny at this temporary post)!

That even on the wind each poem needs
Patience and stillness to be understood,
Like a madman scouring a burning wood
For a drop of water, need no object be
To its physiological lesson:
Impelling organization of the mind
Its lifting leaves upon the drifting wind
Wandering free and far above, as below
The fire of time spreads fast from tree to tree;
The Sibylline leaf sports among the stars,
Hangs from the cosmic branches, restless
Slow, in the wide assumption of thee:
A message of an other world oft poured
The rain most vigorous, with the mind at rest.

THE SHORE

If a fly on a rock
Saw us talking and walking
If an ordained fly
Would see disembarking
Paper boats on a sea
By the wind interacting
Quick arms of amoebas
Contacting, retracting

First bouncing and rocking
The light-folded hull
On the water's lap slapping
Sounds hollow and dull
But as more boats follow
The shudder grows true
With more precious cargo
And numinous crew

A light vessel flounders
On a wavering voice
The silence is louder
The sunshine is harsh
The park shade is further
But the hour still comes
When we will get on
Like organisms

Because the road dips
In the street-crossing spot
By the flashing red dot

Our bodies move not
But in the green ocean
Paper boats in the swell
Say anchor for fun
By strong winds propelled

And though in the river
No foot can be set
Though undrinkable water
The sea's cold and wet
Though summer is failing
All summer we sail
Each word disembarking
To the shore without parting

1630

My dear, I have by turning forks discerned
You are as slow to change as blue-green water
So vast, it holds a sunbeam like a stair,
And hoists the very sky into the air.

The forks fall to the seabed plot,
And a forest in the sand construct;
And a man alone in a wood-sand hut
Muses by a lute beneath the water.

The man, by nature blind and dumb,
Is not deaf, for he plans his days
Around the soft hum in your breast
And turns of sunlight in your breath.

And when the water's very slowly
Rocking air-slips and soft sounds,
And he knows you are asleep,
Then progress he and his lute, unseen

To float on a boat, by the striated shore
Singing like a drunken Greek—
To flowers and goats, to the flaxen moon,
To you if you should hear.

I am not the god of wind; but my voice
Is light enough to ride on air;
Let me sound to you, my very, very dear,
When you upturn your face, when your willow hair

Obstructs enough of life for you to dream

The instant dream, that hollows and makes real;
That panging, piney, air-leak need
Is also music to our ears.

Part ocean infinite, and part discerning smile;
Part god-curled-star, part discarded wine cork;
Part sublime of mountains, part stress ball in a drawer;
Part the trigger-finger lute, part the magic shining beams of moon.

THE RELIGIOUS PERSONALITY

My heart I rupture with impulsive zeal
To think of Heaven's contemplative glow
Dispensed across the light of what is real;
Alas! I raise a doubting mind in show,
A farce of verve, and logic's mimicry;
That mixing with my faith whips up the wind
To sail my paper boat upon the sea,
And ride the world in vast uneasy spin.
Yet when this life withdraws, and all its cares,
And secrets are revealed, I walk the shore;
Devotion's pent and unspent well of tears
Drowns out my cries, and floods my empty core;
Then I sink down myself, and go without me;
And do not doubt the love that lies about me.

APOLLO

O love of Sun, and Light, and Right, and Good!
O power, empty to jettison, but to keep
The green of the leaf, and the brown wood
Like dark the notes of music thrumming deep.

Good night the sun, and now the stars rejoice
With words of light, and whispers of remorse;
The mournful sounds of fountains chorusing,
And the quiet boat with lowered sail at port.

Here the philosopher, the only one awake,
Wanders the empty lane, with feeble torch,
Speaking her thoughts to puddles as to lakes,
Her ardent mind resembles on her crutch.

Yet even she must slumber down to Lethe,
Nor breath, nor word, nor thought without its sheath.

THE LONELY TOWER

There is no place I'd rather be,
Than in a tower by the sea,
On high from where my plaintive voice
Might make the ocean waves rejoice,
If even the waves could make the choice
To dance without the moon;
Nor that the moon would come, and soon
Appear to guide them in their nightly lull,
Whether she waxed or waned, or was at full,
Forsooth she would her rhythm on them foist.

Yet would I ken, when sun was low,
And all the sky was colored so,
In purple, orange, red, and blue,
And at the eve the silent moon
Did peek above the cloud-veil soon,
I held her power to sway;
And that my plaintive music stayed
The tide where it had been of that daylight,
So that evening through, and all throughout the night
The castles kept, we had of building true.

Then would my voice in sorrow's note
Alike the lapping in the moat
Sound pleasant to the little man
Who lived within the town of sand,
And who within his fragile hand
A seashell's fragment grasped;
For he with love had sighed and gasped

The moment we had given him shape and form,
And would his fragment's beauty could adorn
The sandy brow of a little woman.

And he would hear my singing in
The breeze which rudely tore at him,
And even in the crumbling hour
He languished in the sea-weed bower
Laid into love's dream-giving power
Hear my song in his dream;
And hear it in the little stream
I had with whimsy of my finger drawn,
Its bed not deep, but wide and most along
A spring that flowed up from a lonely tower.

Nor would he any ache perceive
When he my sorrow did receive,
Feel greatly in his breast of grain
That nothing solid could attain,
The peeker with his mountain pain
Who kindly looked on him;
He would not see the visage grim
That stared out of the bright face of the moon,
Nor guess that past the sleeper's mighty dune
Came on blue dancers in an endless train!

For every song, though hearts be glad,
No matter be it sweet or sad,
In thinking of us foe or friend,
Though love's dear stream within it wend,
Must one day come to its own end,
And leave us silently;
So I sing my song in the breeze,
And pass well many an hour's pensive weight
With lover's dreams to dine on my white plate,

An appetite my broken heart would mend.

THE WRETCH

Sing, heavenly Muse, and tell me why
I cannot have her, that would be my wife,
Though she complete the fraction of my life?
Why should the feminine spirit of strong verse
A blessing put together with a curse?
Why is the poet loveless and perverse?
For other men are worthy, and not the worse
Who do not hear aright the hidden song
That is the humming of the universe.
Yet why do you deny me simple love,
When love for loving would not deal me wrong?
When I am fit for love my whole life long?
When earth I praise below and sky above,
And my expanding soul for joy could burst?

TO ALBION

The gentle look of frostfruit in the fall,
The furze-flower on its shelf of golden heath,
The aster, bound up in a circle wreath,
And rose ensconced in overshadowed hall,
In a season that endures beyond the year
Describe new weather come in summer late;
The soul in spring, and deep convince of fate
Whose sounds make pictures on my inner ear:
As if the apex of imagined pleasure
No single sense could hold or entertain,
But being all of what we cannot measure,
An echo weaved of past and passionate pain,
Gazed sagelike into time's ambivalence,
Strode o'er the lane, and hopped the infinite fence.

PASTORAL SONNET

In thee, old English countryside, shall I
Aquire my modernness; and shall I grow
To love the city, in a lovely field,
When only hill, and azure sky I know;
And learn of speaking whence the soil till
To speak in seeds that burrow in my soul,
Until the plants, the flower and the vine,
Come up out of the dusty earth below,
And have my "seed-time" in a different age.
Then will I prosper most to fill the page
With lessons learned of tireless equipage;
And like a guileless wanderer return
Into the world less green than sere and dun,
With heavy spirit ripe and harvest won.

THE FORLORN FLOWER

I long for you, til longing turns to grief;
And I close up, despondent, sick at heart!
As feebly able in my self-belief
As a flower from which nectar fails to start,
Despite the workings of an humble bee
Who clasps his wings, and dreads again to fly;
He dreads the rising to the happy tree,
The famished Queen, who question will him why
He nothing makes return; why his quick song
Forlornly sounds, that hurrying should buzz
Of glad and busy life! 'Mid hive's hot throng
How frigid can be, in his own bee-fuzz?
He cannot answer; so works on in vain,
And doubled is the flower's fruitless pain.

LINES ON THE PLATONIC PHILOSOPHY

Once fragrant sipped the dew and stem released,
The arbor bid me with a saving power
That magic was, and from the dawdling creek
O'er waves did minutes sport and shorn the hour.
O precious time! Let none of mystery's bower
Within thee shield; if met we'd meet our search
For Forms aeternal, and sweetness unsoured,
Unshadowed light escaping the dread lurch
And touch and go of meaning's trace and perch;
Of the master bird who sings a master note,
We hear a song from shadows, shadows sing;
Be it pine or oak, willow, ash, or birch,
It is a Tree that sounds in that one's throat,
Be it full at eve, or leafless in the spring.

ON THE SYMPOSIUM OF PLATO

If there is someone who could make me whole,
They must breathe life or death on god's own whim—
A god of love or strife—I do not know—
My disappointed soul connected them.

For, O! how oft, with keening inner-glow,
It seemed me I had found my other half:
Corrective of all loneliness and woe,
Strong wind, and stronger current down below
Would blow my scurvied sadness to the past.

Yet ever was the case, that one I loved
With a passion that could tear the heaven asunder,
Did bolt my soul's soft bark, and send it under.
Is it any wonder that I send no dove,
But strain to hear the sound of rolling thunder?

TRANSLATION OF THE SOUL

If life should pass, when you are stricken down,
Into the sole repository pressed
Of deep reality, where seeds ingrown
With needful soil together find their rest,
Where air, and sea, and sky, and wind unblown
Await their shaping at the hand of glory,
Eternity prepares another story,
And the smiling listener lays the open tome—
Then ever-fast the figures frost and full
Will, like the fragrant olfactory jar
Of incense burned the faithful scroll resume,
Across its page in blots and scars of doom
Your name describe, your mind, and your light soul
Will halo dawn-like on the mountain far;
And when I journey through the night-dark comb
Will hail the boon, a fellow traveler.

TO COLERIDGE

On a certain day in spring, it was so fine
I knew that snows would fall, and dampen early
Those flowers and grasses, which, in copious sun,
Seemed flamelike, and like beauties set in rings
Of alien metal, and ethereal air;
The light so strong which through the green leaves broke
That with a dreading heart I saw it lost,
Delight to pleasance fade, as brown on brown
They from their branches fell, a downward turn
That brought the white up in a dizzying spin;
And winter settled while fall lisped its name;
Settled its breathless comfort over the ground,
And all that had been, went on in a dream
Of quiet darkness, as of life subdued.

NATAL SONNET

Who blooms of water, stems of flowing rose,
The young aye-babbling spring with glittering shows
Sends fountains up in dazzling moonshot!

In time, a sun-blazed flower is forgot
Whose flow and nature turn beneath the earth;
The departed soul, encased in tomes of ice
Restricts the fledgling poet's lyric girth
To lay a lie that lays like Paradise.

Slipping and worn by time, the living ring,
Mysterious, the succor of the east,
In lambswool coat, like winter's secret spring
Greens vibrantly the brown and blasted leaf!

Profoundly he hath stood who stands again:
Philosopher, balladeer, and dearest friend.

DEVOTION

I will be scarce, for you'll have need of me
Before much time has come or living gone;
And though I watch from far, waste not the day
In seeking me in my physical form;
It will not be there, seek you all day long,
Among soft rolling waters where we walked,
Or go at midday, evening, night, or dawn
Along the pathless meadows where we talked
In breathless whisper, ere some other had eavesdropped.

The nothingness I leave you will direct
Your mind in active curiosity;
In fact new-mindedness you will suspect,
The shade that lingers behind every tree
When you would gaze on what you cannot see;
And even the cloudy sky will scan for clues,
Revealed in motions of the shaping breeze:
The sails of boats that crest the world's blue grooves,
Or some great child god, who weeps for missing shoes.

But you will find false clues, and toss them nigh
Distinguishing the wondrous and the true
As the tower of disgrace cannot be high,
No matter if it scrapes the world's blue grooves,
Nor can the detached flower drink the dew;
But sups on sumptuous tears of gratitude,
The elixir conjured for the chosen few
To death consigned by love's vain attitude,
Whether his love he shews, or stands apart and broods.

All you will find untrue, though ever is
Romantic lore that plays in faery land;
You will even come to doubt the goodnight kiss,
The resting shoulder, or the taking hand,
The smiling rainbow in its good wish span;
Until, at even time, you stand alone
A single shadow on the desert's plain,
Where at the full the great moon merely drones
Long light upon cold land, in like somnolent tones.

Then there for me outcall, when life's low scene
Seems harsh and garish in a spotlight mocked;
The tears then poured will travel downward keen
To join soft rolling waters where we walked.
Find out that pathless meadow where we balked
Before love's consummation at a dream,
Still green within your bosom, where we've talked
For utter silence, not implausibly;
And then, my love, my only one, you will discover me.

THE CONJURER

O conjurer! He fills the leaden hours
From light to dark, with words of promised power.
Hiding in his chamber all the day,
He ventures only to the moonlight ray!
And therewith shambles, like the walking dead,
An opal in the center of his face,
And tufts of fire self-shorn from his head
That rise and mix into the airy space.

Doth some spark stir beneath the stair?
Or land amidst the damsel's scuffèd hair?
The conjurer is there beneath the trees;
He makes the homelier hives of the bees!
No puny walk, or stricken tract of mud,
Could flame his escort to the smoldering ruin;
Nor could his diamond heart, or oily blood
Blind the spinster's fingers to the loom.

If traffic halt, or if thy trade be fruitless,
Regard him, poundless, penniless, and bootless;
If thou'rt bewildered, should thy child lean
All groaning like a goat of sour mien,
Remind thyself it is but words he maketh,
He maketh not the ill unseemly winds;
Nor would he coin thee lend, nor any taketh,
Preferring neither enemy nor friend.

Awake at midnight? I say, thou surely art
Caught in the maelstrom of a guilty heart;
The sky thou see'st, big fare of glittering stars,

Make'st moral spelling point a hidden fault;
And even the rising sun, in aspect true,
Allows thee heedlessly, as in a dream
To sleep, still poised at the returning blue,
And brightening of the long-belovèd stream.

If at long last thy ship should run aground,
Thee, and all thy knowledge, go quietly down,
Think not on the blameless one! Who stirs
A hermit-fire and murmurs artless words;
Who has a code of life, and who presides
O'er sunny prospect long of crag and lake;
But go before him, will thy self elide,
And he will thee his boon disciple make.

ON THE 250TH BIRTHDAY OF WILLIAM WORDSWORTH

A great poem is a power from within
That speeds us into stillness, and surprises
The spirit with repose, and with the din
Of worldly dissonance, when it most prizes
Silence, and solitude, and holy thought;
Having scarcity of each, but coming to lorn
Itself partway from thirst, and parting from it
In being something new, something reborn,
For whom the touch of thirst, at first divine,
Is a sacred tool of guidance: now seen the groves
That stand beside the village as its shrine,
In shade the shorn ascetic hardly moves;
Now turned aside, to chase the underflow
Of soul and soil, of heart and mixing loves,
The seed the heart and plant of toiled glow
Made great and green to drink what falls above,
The rains that come, when rain clouds barely show.

And the rainbow finally smiling through the air,
When the blue and red and gold have settled there
Like tresses of the mane of cosmic hair,
When across the space of time such breezes blow
As set all life to order, and make strong
The weak impulses faith resides among;
Then sounds the poet's fair auroral song,
With notes loquacious, sullen, rich, and long,
And by the mind to realms fantastic go.

THE TREASURY OF LOVE

To say, "My heart, she *tremulates* with Love!"
Is to court death, by cardiac arrest;
Yet how else, but by motion-making word
Can I to this new tenderness attest?

Like the dust-wing of a crusted dove
For long years sheltered in a forlorn tower,
She shivers, with the ardor of a bird
On whom insight flashed the airborne power!

But no man, even the poet, soars above
The muddy flow meandering of speech;
To sift the beautiful from the absurd,
Fit words alone can beauty's sermon preach.

So let one coin the dust of worth remove,
And shake away the copper's comfy mold!
Down in the pocket of the beggar's lord,
The penny Love shines like submergèd gold.

And should you find this penny in the grove
Of thoughts that root, and feelings that ensnare,
Spare no expense to care what you afford,
What coin you spend to name its lying there.

And should you find it floating in the cove,
Washed in the waters of the fitful sea,
Christen the ship to bring the lost aboard,
That tremulous the founded Love shall be.

To hold this fleeting thing, this precious Love,

Is such a bliss of terror, and joy of strife,
I must needs stoop to rear a bastard word
That tremulates the trouble strains of life.

THE CREATION MIX

Four little droplets from the sky
Of fire, water, earth, and air
Fell down into a round.
From there across the frozen earth
A fire blazed as in a hearth,
That made an urgent sound.

The fire burned the earth to ash
From valley low to mountain path
And everything between.
When it was done, nor wood, nor dale
Nor ancient tresses heart and hale
Nor anything was green.

But then frothed up a mighty spout
Of aqua firma without doubt
It nourished every wound:
All cold and clear the rivers ran
Across the hateful ember's span
And made the fire drown.

Then came a heavy band of rock
In places that it would elect
To strengthen and make firm
The wishy-washy watered down
And nearly soupy strands of ground
That round its tensors squirmed.

Then blew a master of a wind
With lordlike grace and supple bend

No eye could ever see;
And then came breath and warmth and life,
Love, and death, and power, and strife
And young-eyed Poesy!

THE NECROMANCER AND WILLIAM WORDSWORTH

I am in Hell, and the shadows that transmute
Between themselves the likenesses of minds
Sunk to muteness in the world's dispute
Roil around me. I reach out my hand,
My quivering hand, among the noble soot—
"Where are you?" Over oceans of paged verse
Sought I for one companionable bark;
And restlessly unto the maelstrom drift
Cast forth line and wriggling half-formed pang!
The canon's fired; the shadow giggles through
Each face of each false bard who gibbers truth.
Now sink I in a last resort for you,
And whimper widow's strains of fallen lore;
Wordsworth! Burn I phosphor smeared across the floor.

Such means as this low neon trickles up
To lay on the wide graveyard like fresh snow,
And change the night with faint and terrible glow,
I trust are by no mind easy divined;
When, in the daytime, life, and all its ways
Are as gray today as they were yesterday,
My wicked transmit shines without detect;
And while the castle towns in busyness,
I trawl beneath, a chanting demoness!
Soon, dread poet, shall you rise again,
And make of me, thy one true friend elect;
For the summon salts pulse ready in my hand,

And though what form remains be hardly man,
I can rude Nature even undisect.

And when you must, with deep unnatural pain,
Struggle with loosening arm and flagging wrist,
Again in commune with a deathly Muse,
Who with her basket sifts thy crumbling brain,
And dribbling eyes discover no outward sight,
The untongued mouth hangs round a sorrowing sound,
And the hardening hand cannot the quill make right,
Nor stump of arm and leg through meadow bound,
Yet still must write, I will attend you, dear!
With cant preservative, and ardor that cheers
The hollow in thy breast. O magicked husk!
Outside thy cottage door I busk for ice;
And give to thee, strange god, undying trust;
Whosoever lives beside you, also turns to dust.

LOVE AGES

I saw Love age, I felt her grow,
Her tresses soft as spinner's gold
More white and wan as she evolved
In the cycle yet unfinished;
And though her silvery eyes had dimmed
And their quicksilver irises
Her gaze upon my own did glow
Each pupil dark as bronze had rimmed
With fire undiminished:
So I took her platinum hand, and cleaved it to my breast.

A SILENT FILM

Life is tedious with no sweetheart,
Like a painting but can never dry,
Beautiful without shape or form,
So hesitant to call it art.

When I wake up in the morning,
Before everything else,
I say your name, view your face,
Like a mantra of health.

And when I go to sleep at night
I hold you in my thoughts
Forever in esteem to keep
Suspended over the dark deep.

The interim between
Is aught of suffering—
My spirit runs this way and that
To any wind subject.

But when I go to sleep at night
I pluck the flower's petals
And woo you in my dream
Beside the moon-born stream.

And when I wake at morning
Before first light
I pray that God protect you,
Unto your bed tonight.

Yes life is sad without you,

ADAMNEIKIRK

Like to a silent film,
Having neither sound nor sense,
For all the talking people do.

II: MORE SONGS

2017—2018

A DESCRIPTION OF POETRY

There she lies, with tired eyes,
With a look that's wild and free;
With sunny grace, and stately glance,
With tired eyes lies she.

All day the sunken bed aboard,
Half-strewn with sheet and quill,
Surrounded by the shadows, which
Fall on her as they will.

Who knows that she will come away
From coupling with the dawn,
Her body heavier with dreams
And things to wonder on.

And how she bears the searching grasp,
The hungered hand of night;
When she is burdened with a task,
Her step is soft and light.

A POOR MAN'S FANTASY

If we much time together spend,
As time we do apart,
I would see your face too, my friend,
In the garden of my heart.

To you the little path would wend,
To you the door and stair
Would rise and join the growing bend,
The hidden copses there.

And lo that they should open just,
As at the close of day
The little stars have wise a trust
The sun will go away.

They wait in darknesses who must,
And darkness is their test;
Their linen ashes, and their dust
A fraction darker than the rest.

But lo that they have waited,
All afternoon they've stood
Before the garden gated
Awaiting promised good.

Now evening has abated,
And afternoon is slight;
O enter all ye fated

ADAMNEIKIRK

To climb the hill of night.

CLIMBING THE HILL

O Youth and Hope, spice islands they;
And twin realities of this phantom world!
Never to view except in visions gray
That by their motion seem to be aglow,
Caught with flame by inner rapidness!
And for dim eyes brighter than we can know,
With more work in than machinists can show,
And dipping always on the leading crest
Just out of sight; they make the wide, wide sea
Of life's slow passage haunted with paint light,
Green and gold upon blue currency:
And stand sometimes like two companion stars
Against the double dark of water and night;
When we are lost they show us where we are.

CONSTANCY TO AN IDEAL OBJECTOR

Then one last song, before the open sky
Conducts me chreode-like to England's shore:
Where may have Hartley, in far other climes
Played elfin games upon the lonely moor,
Danced multitudinous through pouring rain,
And legion called out from the kingly tor
The double sound of his dear-given name,
Where heard the smiling friend at Greta's door.
The heart a lee that shelters with its loves,
And not a hollow heart, but with full store
A cornucopia the stranger stoves
Deep in his soul, and there grows evermore;
A place of rest for Earth's sojourning few,
Where carved upon the walls and on the floor
Are signs of welcome, daily pressed anew
To soothe the absence gnawing at the core.
Let no one enter there who does not know
The Muses live, and make the heart adore
A verse both like a river and a road,
That brings us to and feeds the sea of lore.
The sea then grows, and on the rising tide
New wishes flutter and new feelings soar:
That we are more than what we realize,
And ever that which we have been before;
Just like a sea, our souls do ebb and flood;
With poetry we seize the sea therefore,
Scrape tidal diamonds from the ancient mud,

And with a bursting forth of light are poor.

DO SITH DREAM OF ELECTED SHEEP?

"Think not, my young apprentice, of those crypts
Which rest on Korriban, or Tatooine;
Nor even dream of holocrons, and scripts
Of lore on microfilm, in whose thin shine
Deep things are hidden; let what is past expire
Thus in your arms, and let its final breath
Pass through you silently: do not inspire
Of that which long ago went down to death."

"But Master – in my darkest, deepest dream
I stand within those places hallowed now
In our great histories; I breathe the stream
Which like a living power flows around me,
And parts upon its way, as if I were
A jagged rock within it, tall and proud;
And then I feel my destiny, as sure
To my sight as this cowl and this shroud.

Cannot we, who have waited patiently
For years, and bided well in well-earned power,
Who are but Two, by Bane's secure decree,
From far the Order's life-denying tower
Spend but a summer on a boiling moon,
Or winter on some waste beyond the Rim,
In tracing well the dark side's supple frown,
A bloody saga, violent and grim?"

"To purpose what? Your body is my sword.

Would you an academic be? A Sith
Turned scholar? Ha! I give you my fond word,
Make answer thus and you will know my wrath.
The days of war are done: henceforth all war
Will wage through politics; destruction
Will wear the robe esteemed of Senator;
And 'progress' best describe of our Grand Plan.

Begin on Naboo, where your ancient House
Still holds sway in the wake of tragedy;
Be gentle, kind, and wise, and you will rouse
Love and esteem made wanton by pity.
Lure them, Palpatine, with music sweet
Of fortune's promise, and a better age;
Then when the time is right, be not discreet:
Imprison them in an electric cage."

DREAMS

After Jamison Oughton

There is an eye which pictures dreams,
There is an ear which listens,
And every single dream we dream
Has color and condition.

There is of yet no science of dreams,
No true comprised solution,
Except for little songs like these,
Of smallest contribution.

There is a ledger in the soul
For what we cannot measure,
The way the angry ocean's roar
Can give auld seaman pleasure.

And there we write a writ of dreams,
To sort our waking hours
At distance from untiring sleep
Bereft of unsought power.

The dreams of man are wan and thin,
The dreams of moons may thicken,
But 'tis the dreams of gods and poets
Which make the spirit quicken.

The devil has the darkest dreams,
The Savior has the sweetest,

And I have strange and cryptic dreams,
My young Love has the whitest.

These dreams are the gems of Hope
Which dance with mental music,
And pulse in time to solitude's
Strobe of thoughts philosophic.

A poet's Love has hidden souls
Which dance while she is sleeping,
And gaze above his shoulder roll
When his white dreams are writing.

And what a poet dreams, no book
Or diagram may show,
And who it is who sees and hears
Our dreams we'll never know.

EXEMPLAR

For starting in my gentle place,
I hear the rushes run a race,
The willow waves the time obscure
And footprints laid out in a line
Leave many a rhyme the heart can cure
And songs on which the spirit dines;
Leave them floating in the air,
Soft visions of a world more fair.

FOUR FORMS OF LOVE

I am water for you, O cherished friend,
And when we meet beside the river-bend,
Your thirst and heat, I hope to slake and mend.
I am the grasses there, grown green and high,
And when you weary need a place to lie,
Lie down in me, and gaze upon the sky.
For I am that which stretches blue and wide,
The place where clouds and sunny beams reside,
And where the stars are wont to stay and hide.
I am the wind, that pushes planets free
Of their fixed orbits, and through the galaxy
Brings them in boundless perpetuity.
I am the fire, which sparks its ancient light
Across the flint of reason when delight
Makes fair flame dance to woo the sullen night.
I am descent, decay, and even death,
The straggling out the last and forlorn breath,
That lisps the heart to stillness in its cheth.
And I am ocean, full of form and power,
The deepest canyon and the tallest tower,
Who makes a moan, and wanders every hour.
I am the dreams, which in the mind await
To walk you miles in a stranger's gait,
And wink and marvel at a distant fate.
I am the birth that wings all things to life,
The silence in the rhetoric of strife,
The dull but useful handle of a knife.
And I am final pain that only pain

Can burden and awaken, only pain
Can tempt to say, "But it is only pain."
Because I am bliss, invisibly wild,
Bliss which rocks even God to a mild,
And loves, an ageless, formless, childless child.

HOW DO DREAMS BECOME REALITY?

It is hard to have a cold
And not blow my nose.
Because every time I blow
I get mucus in my ear canal.
This is because the ears
Are connected to the nose
(Don't ask me why);
Everything in the body
Is connected, as the body
Is connected to the earth.
From far enough away
The trees are connected
To the sky.

So I must a runny nose
Endure, and attempt
To appease this cold
With Kleenex-compromises,
Jabbing at the superstructure.
Meanwhile I wait, I wait around
For my self to cure myself;
I wait on my other self,
The one that fights infection,
As if it wore a dark mask,
Even before me,
Who loves it best and most,
While the city tries to sleep.

Is this how dreams become reality?
We follow a faerie, and forget
We are sick, and snuffle
Though we shout,
In waiting for redemption,
We ourselves become redeemers;
A will o' the wisp alights
On the edge of a dried-out leaf
And sets it on fire;
The smoke that rises
From the ruined forest heap
Makes the eyes of the clouds
Run over with miraculous water.

THREE BEGINNINGS

I will not melt you, though my love, like light,
A radiant warming parts wherever glanced;
If thou're but a creature made of Fancy's
Fall which slow upbuilds,
I will not teach you thus like water to flow,
Though love's best prize be weeping,
When the sun shines on the snow.

LAURA

Fear not, as you know fate is coming;
Feel fate in strange assorted views
Like golden pieces cut by twos
With severed power richly strumming

That fords a candy, stuck inside
A maze of guilt and fallow field
Nor time, nor time's direction yield
But heat and cold and pain elide

Compressed into a box of pitch
That radiates a feral glow
Stare straight and think of what you know
Do not look at the cackling witch

And dream of Laura, standing there
Her sadness in a field of flowers
No one knows where all the hours
Went, or why the roots are bare

MIRRI'S LAMENT

*Based on the novel
'Rath and Storm'*

In dreams the winds of fate are cruel,
They do not blow for anyone;
In life they blow on silently,
And seem so still when we are young.

A rustle here, and a rustle there,
Nor calms the mind, nor makes it dread;
If something silent stalks behind,
We forward go, and look ahead.

But I have walked the Spirit Way,
And seen a beast with amber eyes;
The beast has told me, I must choose
Which one shall live, and which must die.

My choice is made—for there is one
My heart longs for perpetually;
Yes there is one, I love so well,
That it will be his legacy.

MUSHROOMS OF WESTFIELD

For my Mother

I sat among mushrooms of Westfield
In the park's deep green folds,
Growing imperceptibly older;
I ate the mushrooms of Westfield
In my small careworn study,
Growing imperceptibly smarter;
I listed mushrooms of Westfield
In a late-night meditation,
Growing imperceptibly wiser;
I listed morels and hen-of-the-wood,
The flower-tinged chantarelle,
And heard them speak to each other;
I traveled after rains had fallen,
Around the sigh in the river-bend,
Kneeling under Weymouth pines;
I gathered them in an aged satchel,
Where they lay drowsily
In remembrance of water and soil;
I paired them with bacon and bread,
With grilled onion and hamburger,
And other things which had died;
I used heat to reduce their bodies
And make them lovers of human teeth,
Growing imperceptibly softer;
Their ghostly flavors at the edges
A reminder of the nearness of earth,

That deep taste, fecundly untucked;
While the president memorialized
Fallen soldiers and thanked God,
I chewed a piece of rawhide;
While we dangle over an abyss,
The mushrooms linger in darkness,
Whispering: come to Westfield!

MYSTICAL LOVE

If we love a thing, we will take on its covering,
Though clothing of its essence and our view.
And we may love it without ever knowing
What difference it hides, and that what shows
Is only aspiration or appeal.
Its essence may be opposite complete
The pith of certainty that we call "real";
But what is love, if not essences meet?
Love is a spy that infiltrates the heart,
Through all the walls and gardens of romance;
Comes silently to where their sources start,
A courtier of the mind with rose in hand,
Who suits the door that progress threw askance,
And asks the little lordling there to dance
Shoeless across the stardust in the strand:
Look up at night, and one might see by chance
The detritus of heaven's natal scene,
Which burns to jewelry in the sky's expanse
Fall down like snow, unbidden and serene;
Cover the land, the town, and asking men
Who pray that God will feed or prosper them,
Same street-like strand that runs into the wild,
Conducting hunter, refugee, and child
Into the waiting woods' full quietude,
Place where the birds of winter bless the rood
With songs that winter never understood;
And in the night, by love's side in like dance,
Create the springtime that the world hath needed,

In the deep woods, where birds and children sing,
Upon white snow the hart's pursuer bleeded,
That neither white nor red was covering.

NOCTILUCENCE

These dim-remembered dreams of things to come,
Half-known, half-seen, half-felt, defy precision:
Because poetry's science of exact art
Cannot illuminate a mental dark
Which has been made; it is its own effluence;
And of itself, and of its self-influence
It radiates; and being darkness, glows
To dissipate reality, than show
Some way amid dark willows and light reeds.

And to show Truth by making lies obscure,
Rather than brightly every one abjure,
To tender that small voice and lonely sound,
Moves melodies all soundless into song,
And uses sound to show a hidden world
We had not known for all the brightness here.

Bring me your lamp, the brightest you can find,
Raise high your torch, and I will show you how
There are such shadows as glow brighter still;
Show me with evil works how darkness lives
In the world all light had made, and has perplexed
The very notion of a high design,
And I will look upon you from the depths
Of shadow and of feeling, and that power
Which evening spends upon its slimmest hour,
And take your hand which dreads from confidence.

Then we, like curling ivy on the bough
Of the deep elm, by daylight's closing deepened

With deeply radiance of a noble sorrow,
Will play like polar lights upon one brow,
And make such shades and colors interfuse
As could from all its spectrum tease to being
A world of its own making, all varieties
Of life, and all depictions of the soul
Which go on yet unseen in the bright shadow,
Like sweeter music from a distant room.

NOWHEREVILLE

Have I been softened by these green advances
And made to think and feel in blue romances,
Sure to me the lonely dances come;
At night, when patch of starlight guide my way
I sit and write upon the rising quay
And lonely drifts of waves, so sweet and dumb;
But lovely is it still – they on their way
To Nowhereville, and me on mine to You.

OF STYX AND LILY PADS (MONO NO AWARE)

Stayed up all night to finish my grades,
Beneath a desk light, and the drawn shades
Held back the dawn and Phoebus' attire;
What little crept in, an indigent bolt,
Did fatten itself, a sacrament goat,
Lain on my eyes, a trembling blue spire;
And sere through its crack, a sakura tree,
Surrounded by pines, annoyed by pink breeze,
It shook between, as if it would inspire.

In my mind, a painter's touch:
You sat beneath the sakura and clutched
A lyre on your narrow shoulder-blades;
Staring away to the sky, you strode
Across the strings to the greenly abode,
Your hair as dark as the mists of dark Hades;
And into the fumening narrow you crept,
Where music was, so the lyre had leapt,
And dead lyricists, who had won fair ladies.

Playing a song for the dead, you smiled
A smile that no one could see, and milled
And hobnobbed with the very shades, I vouch;
Like the pied piper, you led forth the ladies,
And with the fair muses made music in Hades,
Beside the god of death on his ivied couch;
The procession from the shimmering ground,
For everything followed the insensate sound,

And when the sunlight hit them, they said "Ouch!"

The sun was rising while I pictured this,
Soothed down to it in my pedagogic bliss,
I slept while red ink on the paper chilled;
As you and the shadows crept up my shoulders,
A general-bard and the thousand toy soldiers,
Each breath I sang out with music instilled;
The sound of the dead, on the living makes war,
When they are asleep, and adream without care,
We are with many loving sorrows filled.

ON WORDSWORTH'S "IMMORTALITY" ODE

In the meanest happening I feel tidings
Not insignificant that seem to ghost
From out of other realms, yet still abiding
Fast in our own, as if gracious to host
Connection, between two unequal worlds;
For example, in the buttons on a shirt,
The choice to loose them, and the shirt unfurled,
Or leave to hold, and make the torso's skirt,
Can give to me a feeling of import
Of something meager set in something great,
Like a banner flying high atop a fort,
Or a fisherman, squat on a frozen lake:
Dualities, and complex facts that make
In the tension that inheres in their whole face
Some greater ghostly power, which partakes
Of ragged outward form and inward grace,
A doublet, made of leather both and lace.

This seems like poet's fate; and yet no theme
Of heaven high, of all mankind, or meaning,
Morality, or life, or lucid dreaming,
Suggests to me with lingual powers teeming
Or in the wordless sounds of Music screaming
So much of life, as of the buttons' leaning
Within their fastening-slots, or else left streaming
The shirt its sides, to hang about my being
Against my chest, my stomach, and my waist;

Tenuous without bond, each in its place
Completely free, but by its form constrained,
Turned on or off by human agency,
Yet differing strands of purpose marry me
To what seems arbitration, small and frail
Ephemera of living, and the thought
That there be some essential in the knot
The button makes to thread its plastic cord;
Some form of me, beyond what I may know,
Beyond the fashion statement, and the show
Refracted in a thousand watching eyes,
And like that net of Indra, which comprises
The living universe, each mirror bursts
With knowledge, nay, with image of its kin,
Each abstract point will form and form again
A second point of insignificance,
Which raises up and glorifies the first;
Just as the scrap of flag anoints the fort,
The fisherman pursues an ancient sport.

This was, I think, the symbol Coleridge saw,
Held in his mind's eye; a natural law
Of how the world unseen bargains for sight
In the witness of the small frame and event,
Of how that which is too vast to depict,
Whose total meaning breaks intelligence,
Confers some of itself, our power be damned!
Into that bit of something which we see,
For in such smallness lies our intimacy,
Soul-precious thing, and solid maketh love,
Rears up, and makes our Love a living breath,
Dear fuel, that runs us straight until our death.

O, does it long? Or did it once, to live?

In the sport of childhood, the giving give
So generously, that even what has not
Intelligence nearly quivers into thought;
The trees become like guardians of our home,
The stones like friendly men we dwell upon
In apprentice pensiveness; the vast blue sky
Is a sea in which the cloudy ships sail by,
And the sea, always a guest, who ever flees,
And waits again to see us, is a friend
Whose haggard garb, and leafy beard suggest
First time the common good of holiness,
So that we find, once we have stood and stared
Out from the sand on gently-glistening waves,
We ever dream again of swaying depths,
When we court sleep in dry unsettled beds;
So like the sea, the sky becomes a man
Who comes around as on a visitation,
And even at night, when all that we called "sky"
Has by soft silent changes disappeared,
And nothing, O! but the weird stars
And idling flames of planets bend about,
Shewing the comets in their flamespit route,
Still there is manness in the universe,
And we learn constellations intervene
Into that chaos wild and serene.

A butterfly which lights upon my hand
On thinly wings displays God's motley plan;
The vast cocoon of what I cannot know,
But must as known hang from a vaster bough,
Has crawling caterpillars for to show,
And ancient noodles for to understand;
Old scraps, and, while the wingèd makes a round,
That like a lily lie on the black bough,

ADAM NEIKIRK

We yet may see the flower in a man,
Who once had entered every wing and stem;
Or see a rose, peradventure, on his cheek,
When he is humbled, or when he is weak,
As when the end of time is choosing him.

ONE WHOM TIMES ELIDE (FOR S.T.C.)

The wide mists of the past I love
To view as from a distant porch
There is a light that burns its torch
Dim round upon the peaceful grove

And in the dark one hears a song
Of relics and of empty things
The silent flutter of soft wings
Is slow and firm of darkness hung

It is hard looking, and hard to see
What life there is in that dark yard
The ground, well-used is bare and scarred
With tracks that move continually

And places in the ground fecund
Impressions made of toil and strife
Great thoughts a moment brought to life
Which a second moment had undone

O there is one for whom I seek
No love no bright nor beauteous bride
I seek for one whom times elide
As the seas elide the forest creek

As the river runs to the sea outbound
His spirit moves in tracts of air
And in dense pamphlets of a sheer
Inconstancy—in language drowned

I grasp life rafts, and feel no bank
Of sand beneath my kicking feet
But seem to smell sea salt and peat
And burning ridges long and lank

And hear the mourning dove's sad call
Yet unreturned at evening's break
The sun sinks down into the lake
The stars some mystery yet appall

O father-spirit! Rushing guide
Who makes the weeds and rushes bend
Like the midnight's sudden wind
Comes up over the mountainside

You make these fibers and these ghosts
Release their scent to my glad nose
That purpose offer and repose
To knowledge's unresting hosts

And to me even, sipping time
Hold out the cup of drowsing drink
Who more than any make me think
And out of thinking build a rhyme

Who stand beside my bed at night
A model of humanity
And show me what it is to be
Fraught much with demons as delight

RETURNING TO HAMMERSMITH ON FOOT

To cut my fare in half I make my way,
To save nine shillings, on a woodland path;
And though around me pleasant streamlets lie,
As thro' them, Sun, darts his fragmented eye,
And birds on branches, in their hushèd tones,
Sing while the fire of love reminds their bones
The lightness they might bear, to take to wing,
Who wait for early, to be middle spring,
I feel nine shillings in a money pouch
Make up for hopes unbreathed and honeyed touch;
That my old shoes, that by the passing day
Grow older, and unkinder to my feet,
Have taken knowledge, aye, the wisdom's way,
No London alley, nor expressive street,
Into the cracks that seam their eventual defeat;
And hold themselves together for the ward
That lives in them, whose childish peace they guard!
Children who once, in even younger days,
Did dance all naked in the wildest scenes,
Up on the hills, where flies and garden snakes
Hidden behind them passing, sight unseen,
And side by side, like dancers, followed down
As blind as rivers to the mighty sea.

I have nine shillings which the cobbler will,
When these sad jaunts the foster parents kill,
At last! The rain beside the cobbler's door
Falls on new orphans by the cobbler's awning,

ADAM NEIKIRK

Who have no art to await his mending skill,
Or sight to see the eastern light returning,
But shiver madly thro' the dark of night
Who once beheld it, and without affright,
Steal softly down the shoulder of a hill,
And deaf the music of the summer's ear.

REVERENCE OF THE INVISIBLE

"The first introduction to thought in the transfer of person from the senses to the invisible. The reverence of the Invisible, substantiated by the feeling of love – this, which is the essence and proper definition of religion, is the commencement of the intellectual life, of the humanity" (STC, OM, 2:78-79).

Hidden presences—we feel them most,
Alas! Our foe to stain with motive's ghost,
Imparting spirit to a fleshly thought,
The veiling bones of an auspicious plot;
Or else a styled curtain, which deceives
The patterned omen even as it weaves
Our fate in darkness; that all fate is dark:
We see the flood before we know the ark.
That all we see not is—invisible:
Too small to see, inconsequential—
Equivocates our essence; absence fills
Us not with that due reverence, which it wills;
But tends to lone us, as the desert's lore
Distills the dune, and on each sandy tor
Each grain outpours with sorrow all alone!
It adds its number to a sum of one.
Nor sees the mighty dune it rides, as drops
Of falling rain see not the sun-bright tops
Of cloud far higher; who but, descending,
At most, in streams all seaward wending,
Espy reflections of the thunderhead;
And think their falling is a sign to dread.
What else but love has starry eyes to see
Those constellations of our destiny?

What other sight but love's may dissipate
All sounds and shapes into a single fate?
But teach the grain, the raindrop once to love,
And they will walk on beaches of the cove;
And in eve's darkness, love's translucent light
Illuminates a telescope of light.

But how to act upon the Self: disperse
This battle-book, into a page of verse?
A line of thought, like sunlight from a star,
May pass unseen, the lens of who we are;
What is the organ fitted to detect
Those strange conclusions that the mind rejects?
The heart, which ruled us once in childhood,
Now like a hermit in an old pine wood
But stirs a little fire, yawns, and flings
To wolves the scraps of merriment he sings
In hours of drunkenness; his downturned face
By his own comfort seems to be disgraced,
And glows with hollow shame; his sadly garb,
Grown leatherly to stem the idle barb,
Is like a second skin; and of his name
Is all but dispossessed—his only claim
To memory is the outline of the sound
Or shape of what it was, as when the ground
Which we have thrown upon our buried dead
Conceals them, we will suffer not to tread,
Because it imitates the buried tomb.
And yet the heart is quiet as a bomb:
It makes no warning of its going off,
But as the old man pauses now to cough,
May suddenly be roused to detonate
By those fair forces which in heart had sate,
And bid it stir its fire in secrecy.

Such is the love of what we cannot see;
This love extends into the space it makes;
And for all spacious mystery it wakes
A way of being present heretofore
Unknown to us, and to a further door
Self-furnishes the key. Then life is strange,
Not frightful; its experiential range
Is awesome, not bewildering; for as all
That once had chaos been and idle lull
Confusing of our inner-sense, and of
Our static expectation is, by love,
Transformed into an alphabet of odd
Responses to a world suffused with God,
We love ourselves—as readers; and delight
Letters, then words, then sentences to write,
To con divinity with wild script
Faultless we fail to render its description,
And find that failure is a way to live;
Daily our hearts and minds of failing give
The better of themselves, until the day
They have no more of them to give away,
And like proud stones, into a silent lake,
Skip once and down into perfection sink.

SCAFELL

When you see the seams and holes in everything,
The arms of the blanket one wraps tight is a ghost
With a long, tattered shawl and hidden face
In the space beside your uncovered head, waiting.

Waiting for? But the aim of the ghost is to wait,
Looking ahead with its almost-eyes, thinking slow,
Careful thoughts about the feel of the floor.
My life seems like a suicide waiting to occur,

Many times on some days will I weigh options,
Why just yesterday I imagined taking my books
And gathering them into a pyre and setting down
All tired and jubilated to swallow matches,

To go up with a million mournful black letters.
It seems like the perfect time: alone and single,
Nearly 30, pre-diabetic, he would have appeared
At his second conference in England this year

To talk about Coleridge's *Biographia Literaria*,
Published two hundred years ago;
And to hike slowly and with great discomfort
To the top of the tallest mountain in the Lakes,

Which I believe is Scafell: not even in the running
For world's tallest mountain. And probably to
Read poetry after we have all had our dinner,
To commit faux pas because I did not read Wordsworth,

But, hoping for more book sales, read my own.

It's called *Songs for the Dead*, and it's on the table
Or it's in a box under my chair, or it's in my bag
Under my bed in the five-person dormitory,

And you can have 24 of my poems for $15,
Which is sixty cents a poem, about five cents a line,
Because a lot of them are sonnets, and when
I was in England last year I wrote forty sonnets,

Though most of them are still on my phone,
And now because I am dead, I suppose that no one
Will ever read them. And I must confess
The sincere wish that my death not make me

Famous, for I would have preferred to be famous
On the strength of my writing, and not because
I was an interesting character who happened
To notice that I was an interesting character.

Perhaps that is what suicide is: self-recognition,
A way of finally speaking to one's own self,
And though it deal in pain and blood somewhat,
A language that the body can understand.

Does that make it right? Does it matter?
I think in my best light, I was a moral philosopher
Without any real philosophical training,
But someone with both head and heart enough

To have an intuition about what is the best life,
And what human beings needed to be happy.
And that was how he knew, someone wise (but
Terribly clever) will say in the near future,

That he wasn't happy, that he didn't have
The things he needed, and that in itself is enough

To justify what he did, for in the end, all
Is self-knowledge, all moves us inevitably

Toward the top of the mountain-top.
And it was Coleridge who went to the top
Of Scafell, and looked down across the abyss
At the lakes and strumming shadows there

And who wrote in his oilskin notebook
Such beautiful things about the shifting clouds
That we almost forget how close he came to
The edge of the top of the mountain where he stood.

SCENE OF THE CRIME

Here lies a poet: see, he's dead!
The crime is done, here lies his head
Of power, passion, and dreams bereft,
His voice is silent, and nothing more
That we can say will start his breath;
Though we to all the gods implore
That he should live on as before.

We only have what songs he left us
Before his quiet passage reft us,
Before the spirit of doubt and shame
Threw dirt and duty on his name,
And cast the final chaplet to the floor.

O heaven above! Pity us, and send us
Another who will praise and mend us,
Who'll sing our songs, and make language dance!
Then we should roof him, guile and feed him
Sweet stuff to stuff him full of laughter,
And also take him round, and breed him
With every politician's daughter,
That there might be a race of writers hence!

At last we'll set him up a living
In Highgate or in Piccadilly
For when his honored years are many,
His verses brief, profound, and silly,
We'll do our part! For humans being
Need poets as they need their breathing.

ADAM NEIKIRK

For every poet born they say
God pressed a thumbprint on the clay;
For every poet in the ground,
God weeps and weeps and can't be found
In heaven for a day or so,
And the angels don't know what to do.

SELF-LOVE

What is self-love?
What a strange little thing.
It isn't part of us;
It's more like a ring
Which we can take off
Or put on as we choose,
Like a favorite sweater,
Or an old pair of shoes.

So it shouldn't look "good,"
But it should look "right,"
Like it isn't too loose,
And it isn't too tight.
And should be seen on us,
Wherever we roam:
In the blades of green grasses,
Among the tombstones.

And it should stay on us
All through the long day,
And fade to each glimmer
Of the sun-ray;
And only at night,
When the stars are aloft
With those whom we love
Should be taken off.

For we needn't adorn it,
When the people who love us,
Like guardian angels

ADAMNEIKIRK

Have gathered above us.
And needn't protect it,
By our tender keeping,
When we and our loved ones
Are quietly sleeping.

Then where does it go?
It lays in a drawer,
Beneath a slant thatcher
All covered with snow;
And waits without thinking
For the glorious morning
When it will be needless,
Worn only for wearing.

THE BLUE SHIRT

I have to take the shirt down from the hangar
Choosing the grid-marked button-up in blue
(Hoping to square my thoughts and make them true)
For when I sit and write my thoughts of you—

It is unknown to me, someone in a dark fog,
Who might imagine the soul hung on a stick
Like an effigy to frighten crows and ravens,
If what I think I know, or feel, (feeling for
Meager portions of a heart not grown sick,
Which might, without this long apprenticeship
To craving, and to simulated loss,
Throw up its petals, beat and make a haven)
Is really anything other than
The fog left on the mirror, and the wit
Of a hand, not mine (or is it?), which hand
Appears out of a fog I did not make,
Appears always, wherever doors should be,
It takes my breath: from out of breath constructs
A beautiful image, of a beautiful land,
Where ought to be, a way to pass beyond.

Can I put on my blue shirt and reduce
All inner-chaos to a perfect plan?
If shapes are primal like Pythagoras said,
Can I pull pincing squares out of my head?
And if I do this, indeed, if I am
Momentarily poetic, what span of time
Until they burst, and all this graceful rhyme
Go spilling forth and crossing back again?

Then there will be clothes all over the floor—
Dishes of candy on the kitchen table—
I will reach unable for the beauteous door—
And cry a little in the beast's small shell,
A crocodile with a purple skull.
Even if we had kissed upon that spinning wheel,
My friend, I am afraid I would not feel it—
Though all of life be moments pictures may tell,
'Tis only words that square us, men with Hell.
How prettily one whispers from a haven
Where, heartless, one may think and plan it all,
No haven made from heart's soft-beating wall,
But made from armor, plates that nary fall.
Though saying that word, I smile, that soon leaves
Will streak across the sky and cover the earth,
Sweet earth, that once seemed mine to walk as well;
That seem like colors where the earth had grieved;
And colder days will come, that will in-birth
Some faint primordial dread in wakefulness;
Then as they tread in emptiness and gloom,
But seasonal, for it will fade and pass away,
To paint a picture of a blooming tree,
I will make murals of a fine spring day,
And hide them even from the falling snow,
Behind the plates that make the turtle seem to glow.

THE FADING STORM

Poetry is a storm which passeth through
Each man his sky (though some may narrow wonder
With a blinking and insignificant eye
Why rain is fewer and the scraps of thunder)
In his youth, used to rage's several winds
Grown big and booming on the far, wide sea
It even shatters islands with its mount
Where might have made the land on destiny.
And keeps him soft propelled in middle age:
This is the score for those who play the part;
And hearing peals of blue electric bells
When others hear the faint continuous heart's
Living refrain; and making mighty surges
Of battle-charges out of life's main dirges,
And making wildfire out of flame,
And like cathedrals from his written name.
I only have to wonder left to me,
What it will be when I am old and well;
When some young stripling reads my poetry,
What color will she listen to the bell?
What will her silver say when I am gold;
Will I sound like the storm when I am old?
Or will I be the walking make of calm,
Who saw the great deluge and heard it pass;
Who listened with the rest to silence now,
And to her sound as silent as the rest?
This lass will know me as a failure. Yet,
I write for her, I lift her on my shoulders,

ADAMNEIKIRK

That she may see beyond the fallen towers,
The storm which fades into the distance set,
Oft grumbling yet, and mumbling yet and yet.

THE HOOK

I cannot write a poem with a purpose;
I cannot write one that would win a prize
(It isn't that I don't feel I deserve one);
I cannot write a poem that has eyes

Embedded in each letter to observe you,
Thou patient mine, and to obtain your heart;
If this to thee works on like medicine,
It was not made such healing to impart.

For these are nothing but that moment fishing,
That moment when the hopeful line is cast,
When neither fisherman, nor fish is wishing,
The other had not so much pressed his case.

If you ask the hook that flies into the ether,
It will tell you: I have never heard of bait;
I do not know why animals are eager;
I do not know why that man sits and waits.

I suppose I do not mind this wormy offal,
Nor the open maw that hides my crooked sheen;
But the plunge I make into the dark is awful;
And I miss the days when I was warm and clean.

THE OLD MILLENNIAL

The old regard "the world today"
As a heartless fiction nigh derailed
They watch it like a crossing train
Flown over sand and sailed away

And at the bottom of the drink
Rusts the car with spinning wheels,
Around our head the glass grows thin
As what we breathe, we feel.

But the young will see the dragon fly
On solar-powered wingèd steel;
And sing like birds the busy sky
From the autoautomobile.

Better to turn away, says I,
And tend to my quiet zeal—
Suddenly middle-aged, I die
Between the water and the reel

Which God, it seems, dropt from the sky
Good as his children's weal;
A line of fiber, as a golden eye
Might drop a silver tear.

Where all hath ended, these begin
With hope and precious claim,
The young are like a vanish'd tide
Bright as the noon and a mile wide
Returning whence it came.

How could they understand the rules

Who scorn to play the game?
O let me with my cane disguised
On a surfboard smart to surf itself
Go with them in the evening light
A man among the elves;
I'll hide my tempered beard and sun myself
In a vanity they do not recognize.

THE SEA OF SADNESS

Like many things, the sea is cyclical;
The sea of sadness has its ebb tide too.
The crystal waters rush and make a gladness,
Then pull away and leave me feeling blue.
My challenge is: to stand upon the sands
In heat, and in soft clouds that hide the day,
Look out and love those long uncastled lands
The sea of sadness came and took away.
And not to think, when I see children play
That all their labors make them sinful kings,
That empty dowers to Poseidon pay,
Who only brings them sorrow in the sea;
Or that all ends as it began: in clay,
All they, the builders, and the sea in me.

THE SPARROW AND THE CARDINAL

For my Grandparents

Black cherry and black walnut
Their tempers side by side
Stretch out in veillike solitude,
Their tempers override.

A sorrow on the sweet birch
Sours the sugar maple,
Like smoke upon the white ash
And white on the black willow.

A shadow on the sassafras
Vines o'er the dogwood's flowers,
And the bitternut hickory tree
Discards his dismal dower.

The tulip and the poplar
Hoptree and sycamore
Quake gently as the aspen,
On Hudson's peaceful shore.

And know the sunny hornbeam,
Red oak and yellow birch,
Grow softer in the shadow of
The sparrow's empty perch.

But only in one beech tree
Crouched near the grasping ground

ADAM NEIKIRK

On his low-springing branches sat
A red-plumed cardinal.

And he had loved the sparrow,
This cardinal from the south,
And when he sang without her
Her song was in his mouth.

For he so loved the sparrow
He had traveled to the north,
To sing a lay for Hudson
Where the passage sullied forth.

And through the winter wind and snow,
Clasped in the tree's bare branches,
He sang beside the sparrow's perch
The emptiness enchanted.

And when he sang without her,
Her song was in his mouth,
So that every passage falsely told
Still carried us to else.

Now carry on the passage,
It is the cardinal's way,
Who sings the sparrow and the sea
To the sound of Hudson's Bay.

For there are rites of passage
That do not end in time,
And as the dead have noticed us
We notice them again.

And as they, loves tremendous
That do not end in space,
The sparrow and the cardinal

Each in the other's place.

THE SPOON

Space and time deliver us – how does inspiration 'strike'?
For me, I feel many things at once,
Both thought and feeling, almost as if they warred
Like two sparrers, with two different kinds of sword,
Full with their need and envy, but unable to connect.
Thought with his logic quickness, aye, and the broad
Cold metallic blade; feeling wields a shaft of gaseous green,
But barely weapon, that o'erclouds and pulls
Its strange strength from the very atmosphere; and they
Simply wear themselves out in hitting without purchase,
Missing without fail. It has taken me almost thirty years
To get over the pointlessness of their battle, and to love
Instead the desperation of a victory that can be
By the long expertise of multiple assured failures
Foretasted; like a disappearing soup,
The taste of the spoon alone which one grows to love.

"THE TWO SISTERS"

An adamantine chain, that Kant had spun,
That old Kant! Shuffling through my faery story;
'Midst rainswept fronds of Königsberg he suns,
And waits these lines to seize upon his glory.

And writing about Coleridge, who dis
Inherited himself in form and face;
As adamant a chain, as Kant had spun,
Combines his weakness to my carapace.

To write a poem, badly made, but aim
Love's balding arrow at a pretty lady:
"O heart! Fond heart!" – the bowstring as it twangs;
No one can blame it if the heart's unready.

But publish it, and they will have a row.
Those—those surrogates! How dare he make the stand!
Who once, to fight the bloodless war of Christ
Did pledge all three of his head, heart, and hand.

He should be in the Lakes, atop a Scafell;
Or in the West beside the Holford combe!
Why does he fan his hand to waft the musk
Half-settled in the garland-empty tomb?

This stench of his, anathema to amarynths!
Why does he not least mask it with perfume?
I'll quickly rect a sunny pleasure dome
And stock with demons, lyres, and the Moon.

Come right this way, and see that genius weaved

In magic circles, fed on honeydew!
Meanwhile the self-exile will feel the chill
Beside the Otter, in the land of few.

But should he, half-reclined upon the ice
That he himself had built in pleasured madness,
Be left alone to write on what he will,
He'll turn again to love, that happy sadness.

With infinite pictographies of Asra
Spread out like coffins on his ankles crossed,
This giant will tie corpses to his fingers
With golden strings as delicate as floss.

But not to make them dance, or bat an eyelash
To flutter kisses on his tear-soaked cheek;
He'll drop a match upon his greatest poem,
To make a hearth around for them to speak.

Then rising with a universal sigh
(I told you Kant was watching from afar)
Far rather would he sit in solitude,
And leave the little Asras as they are:

With brooding, flocking, and marvelous winging,
To coo and cuddle themselves, and all they own;
But feels a holy pang to hear them singing
His travels up the mountainside alone.

THERE IS NO LIGHT

There is no light which does not find its eye,
However small, and tenuous, and slow;
The weaker, yea, to see and wander by,
The more of fire does an iris show.
And when the flowers blaze with summer glory,
Spring spirit in the soil, and warmth compact,
Who've risen freely without plotted care,
But only nature's educated act,
The heart commands a reverence for that story,
And slows to wonder at them, where they are.
So do I wait with overflowing soul
Where what dry day innocuously yields,
As if so unaware the rain had flown
The cloud perched heavy over grassy fields.

UNENDING WINTER

It's cold today, but at least the sun is out,
And bathes the ungrown grass and the bare trees
In a yellow light, like the light of memory
Diffused to the world from its personal chamber.
In this shared light, whose connection to the mind
Must be so fragile, I can see into
The future by my knowledge of the past,
Viewing summer as it was in childhood.
Beneath the tiles and weeds I see beaches,
And in the sound of passing cars hear oceans
Roar, then retreat; filling in a moment
The spirit like a sail made full with wind.
The weatherman who sends the faculty
Near-daily updates and predictions
Calls it "unending winter"; every week
Another storm looms on the near horizon,
The sad and angry faces of strangers
Aye populate my social media feed
As snow falls all around them, and they weep,
Or curse the invisible empire of the air.
It is the situation we find ourselves in,
Investigating the power of black holes
In giant underground atom-smashers,
Flummoxed by the weather of our own world,
Convinced that, lifeless, thoughtless, and mindless,
It holds us in a bond of cruelty,
Settling its vendetta with late snows
And the flush of warmth perpetually delayed.

The shovel we have built, once so profound,
And made profounder by painstaking work,
Seems now in ever-winter shallow, coarse,
Retrieving less and less of the snowy mounds
Which border us like mountains; and the cave,
Which we had stumbled from in wisdom's glare,
Is warm, and full of knowledge. "Let's go there!
If only for the time that winter lasts."
And there we go into another world,
By page or screen, or hidden sonic bud
Like to the ear, a world where the sun shines,
And we stand on the prow of an old ship
With salt and sand muse through untroubled hair,
And every drop of sweat that does not fall
Is like a piece of silver in the main,
All vast and blue with many dancing pockets.

TO BE A TREE

If I have a special talent, it is to be a tree;
My skin embarks and my limbs grow leaves—
Like a wereman in moonlight, nearly new,
But just a crescent – is when I bloom.

As my body makes it treewise,
My tree limbs make flowers,
Whose petals fall around me
In sensory showers.

I grow my roots into the earth, and stand
In the times that try men's souls:
I merely laugh! With soundless mirth
I pierce the eternal.

And I know that the great sun
Is something strange and very far;
But it is like the engine
And I am like the car.

Or rather, photosynthesis;
The sun is like the oil;
Combustion, or at least the gas
Which makes the fire boil.

And what am I? My human buds
Don't hear me when I speak in tree;
And worry me, for I was
Reported missing yesterday.

Yet I am four feet from the room

I used to live in as a man,
And can still lay my leafy shade
On the place I laid my head.

Yet now I see in dreamfulness,
What I once momently
Saw for a portion of the night,
The surface of the sea.

I live in dreams: the dreams of men
Which they will visit time to time,
Within the crib, and not again
Until they're old and dying.

WORLD OF DIAMONDS

I.

I miss the days, sometimes, when it seemed
That everything I said had a sole meaning,
And my intentions were like my being:
Whatever I was, that I could be deemed.

The world too, in those days, had only one
Star, which by its light, for each thing alone
Cast one shadow wherever it shone,
And of other stars, and other shadows, there were none.

But shall I tell you now where I come from?
A world composed of shadows, and each one
Has a small sun inside its vaporous bones,
A light to find, whose source is hardly won;
One spies though dimly, through a swirling glass,
And sees more shadows from the shadows cast.

II.

A world of diamonds!(?), that one finds at night;
Each one restores its gemmatic twilight;
Casts longer shades upon the fading ground,
And disappears, at dawn, without a sound.

And when the heart is a diamond, in the dark,
We hurt, and bleed, to touch it so stark;
We cut ourselves—until we harden, too,
And our touch then cuts the gentle and the true.

Forgive me then if that is what I've done;

Conditioned to see stars in every corner,
And shadows wrapping over everyone;
The time has passed that I have been a mourner
For the simple world that wisdom took away,
A world that simply is too good to stay.

III: COLCHESTER

2019—2021

A LETTER TO STONEY, COMPOSED 27 NOVEMBER 2019

(As I have been writing almost every day
In pentameters, it seems fitting to form
My letter to the same rhythmic display;
Sometimes it will not rhyme, sometimes it will,
When significant facts - and what is not? - require
To show themselves in more poetic attire,
And more musical verse.)

          The east of England
Is humid, being near the sea, and cold,
And the sky is always covered with grey clouds;
The architecture of this place - I mean
The University of Essex - seems, to one
Newly arrived, and with an eye hope-full
Of Albion's famous greenery, at first
Repulsive, and the polar opposite of that
We think of when we dream of the 'green isle':
From the brutalism of its concrete buildings,
The insistent modernism, which recalls
Socialist movements of the 60s and 70s,
The towers named for Morris, Keynes, and Russell,
Rawley, Tawney, and Eddington; which creates
A penal feeling, an insistent pull
Guiding the body between walls of iron,
Or cells of glass and plastic, shaded lanes,
Leading to deeper places, pavement, steel;
I stood out in the drizzling rain and thought

That I had been transported; my mind ran
Over the list of my past indiscretions,
As I pushed my suitcase along the hilly road
And after thirty hours awake, at last
Dropped myself off in my accommodation.

I live in the Meadows, there, in Conway House,
A postgrad house, one of a few
Doctoral students, among Masters students,
Whom I over the next several days
Had cause, or chance, to meet, and did befriend,
Until they soon became the natural glue
Which by affection tied me closer to
This campus and this university.
My room is small -- too small to be believed!
It is dominated by a double bed
(Four feet wide, I am told, and eight feet long)
And a walkway near the bed, which turns to the right
To form an L: along the lowest limb
Of that imaginary letter, is
A wardrobe which I cannot move; and a desk
Bolted into the wall, upon which rests
Most of the things I now own. And in the wardrobe
Are all the clothes I own: most brought from home,
A few things purchased here, at discount rates,
Some jackets, trousers, long- and short-sleeve shirts,
Sweatshirts, etc., and my hat and scarf,
Which I almost never leave the room without,
Are laying on the desk near where I write.
I have water bottles, weights, diabetic
Medication, a vase on which is depicted
A rural scene, a windmill, birds in flight,
A wireless mouse, a guitar, which is not
Mine—but borrowed from a friend some weeks

Ago, and never yet returned; and of course
A binder filled with poems, which I have not
In any event, had any course to use,
And have not opened.

                    Then there is the bathroom!
'Tis said, an airplane's gives more elbow-room;
Between the walls there is not even three feet
Of space; one showers in a straighten'd way,
And does one's toiletry, and hygienery,
As in a plastic box—at least the shower
Is not too fitful; the door closes and locks;
But the floor is always wet, and one takes care
To step most carefully when wearing socks.
No more of this; it is a subject grim.

I must confess, my days are given over
To writing in the morning, and at night
To socializing. I have begun a long poem,
My biography of Coleridge, to be called
'Your Very Own Ecstasy'; just today
I will, for the first time, visit my guide
Dr Adrian May, who is due soon to retire;
I have a team of supervisors, but thus far
Have only met one of them once; and I
Do not have classes; I have no obligations
(At least that can be easily referred)
Except the ones I make upon myself,
And this is the task the school did trust to me
When I sent in my research proposal.
Each day, for three days in a row, I rise
And go to the Albert Sloman library
With my flash drive, and up to the fifth floor,
Which is the floor given over to English writing,

And sit at a computer, and produce
Fifteen hundred words of blank verse, then cease
Until the next day, and begin again,
For three days; then I spend a day without
Any writing. Since October the 19th
I have toiled sensibly and vigilantly
To meet my words each day, and also to rest
In needful silence, until, the night of which
A day I have not written, I can feel
(Thank god!) the afflatus at the ready again;—
I now have almost forty thousand words,
Almost half of what I was meant to write within
Three years of study; but still I have not flagged,
Tho' I confess, again, that on Thanksgiving Eve,
I am homesick, and wish I could join you all.

What of the poem itself? So far detailed
I have of Coleridge's early years; almost an hundred
Pages of his childhood have I written alone,
Blending fact with fiction, unto a myth
Not too explanatory—for childhood is
Strong in our making, but not everything,
It does not make us all; it forms a part;
And so I after some expanse of time
Moved on from there, and left a page all blank,
And jumped ahead to the voyage to Malta,
Coleridge in 1804, aboard the *Speedwell*,
Full of regrets and hoping to perish
In a storm or sea-battle between the French
And Algerians and the southward English fleet.
Still he is haunted by the one he loves,
Called Sara, or Asra, or Asahara,
The 'moorish maid' who dominates his mind

And fills him with strange visions, which dissect
His living experience and make it but ensconce
The image of her; O! it can be piteous.
But there are still another thirty years
To follow him, to turn about and view
The mind within itself, and shew that thesis
That the best part of our language comes from when
The mind describes its action to itself.

And what else? I have met young people from
All over the world; from China, India,
Japan, Spain, Greece, Cypress, Turkey, and France,
From Italy, America, and England;
All alike in programs (at least to me): they are
Masters of Science, studying economics,
Or data science, or biotech, or finance,
People who hope to seize their degrees in
A year, or two at most, and then to work
And live on in relative comfort; there is not
That sense of dread, and calmlessness, which pervaded
The classrooms of my teaching in the States.
The nihilism of the United States
Does not exist here; I have barely found
The cynicism, and irony, of home,
Which marked so many, which marked the minds of men
And women of my age, and which marked me,
And made me dread society. But there
Is an openness that I have never found
At any time before; and I am glad
They want me, some an outsider, 32,
Studying (who?) this poet, and creative writing,
To join them in their efforts and their leisures.
The Italians call me "The Novelist"; they expect
My drinking and my smoking, and sometime

They give me recommendations for writers
I have never heard of; and I try to explain
Why I feel the world needs Coleridge at this time;
And there is one, from Catalan, named Marc,
Who with me deplores our present situation,
Our neoliberal post-modernist bent,
And gave me a book, called *Lord of the World*,
Which he believes will make me a conservative
(Although I have already attempted to explain
That just by believing in an 'human nature'
I am conservative). Marc briefly loved
(Or perhaps it was not love, but here's a poem)
A woman, Sarah, from America,
And dated her about a week, until
She broke it off; but now they are restored
At least to friendship, if to nothing more;
And sometime such has happened to others
Among our circle, where for a brief while
Romance has made them closer, or further apart.

But I must sadly hasten to the end
Of this first letter, though there is much unsaid,
Much that needs fixing, much that could be better
Explained, like all the locales of the campus,
The tone of it, the strikes by the UCU,
The city of Colchester, and the dangers of that place,
And nearby Wivenhoe, a fishing-village,
And the Indians with whom I talked of Vishnu,
And a girl I met, or girls; and how it is odd
That I have written so much in isolation,
And barely without speaking of it to anyone,
And not lost heart. Yet even now I go
(I give my 1500 words today to you)
To meet with Adrian and see if I

Have made some grievous error, or if he
Will approve of what I've done . . . am I a student?

Please send my love to those you'll see today:
To Lee, and Chauncey, and my mother and father.
And if they care to, they can read these lines!
And I will call you later, and we can talk
Whene'er there's moment, around the dinner table.
And I am sorry, I have not written before,
But that my life, has rushed around my mind
Like a tide around a man who's learning to swim.
But I have thought of thee often, and am glad
I had time today, in the spirit of Thanksgiving,
To send you this imperfect poem-account
Of a small part of my doings. Until next time.

A RIVER RIPPLING OVER THE SAND

A river rippling over the sand,
A ruined tower on a rock above,
A promontory, and a mountain-ash
Waving its berries. How am I to express
The exactest nature of this swirling current,
These quivering motes, those darkening starlings?
All world is a process: similarly
All the world is a series of imagined things.
And all the world, that is known to us
Be but surfeit of symbols, and surfeit
Of the meanings of these rare translucent things:
The picture of fame on your smiling face,
The sound of luck that lingers in your hair,
And the motion of the wind behind your eyes…
Combine to show me, in your step, your gait,
And in the prattle of your prattling voice,
A picture of my thanks and my regret,
A mellow jungle in a city of bone.
Ars! Poetica!

Imagine a god-like thing that loves you so
It nearly smothers you; always drawing near,
Wanting to touch you, talk to you, & overhear
Your every waking thought and each of your dreams;

Always touching, framing, alongside
Your body half your spirit and wanting more;
Until at last you cannot take anymore,
And you take this immaterial thing that says

"*I'm yours*" and tear it limb from vanished limb;
And stamp it out, like so many pieces of
The refuse of a day. At night you lay
In the long deep drip of peaceful self-solicitude
In the long unending tunnel of human life,
Moving toward a light that seems to move away.

ASRAEL

Aye he hath stood

But did he stand hard?

Like that pine grove
By a castle huge

Where nightingales sing
Of a summer's eve

Or like St. Bart's
Anciently ensconced
Among dead meats?

Dura Navis—that meaneth
A Hard Ship

When Christopher
Wordsworth drowned
He would it had been him

Aye, he hath stood
Alone together
With the madwoman

He hath passed slowly
Over empty fields
Trew meadows of the same

Written comfort
In the ink that pour
From human heaven unconcealed

Made a game
Of playing a game
During a different game

Who is he? I say
We all know his name

The kingdom of god his poor
Repeat after me

Aye he hath stood
Softer than before

He hath loved the miserable
Puddle in the road

And the little birds
Hopping beside the hedge

He hath shivered with
Anthropocenic dread

Who is he? I say
He belongs to all of us

Not like the Genius
Visited upon few

The Commanding Genius
Which visiteth some

And that True Verity
Who comes to even less

The Good Life
Not many have got

And all the wealth of Scotland

At the rainbow's end

The wall we see each day
The prison house
The block

None of these have stood
Aye, but he hath stood

Line a fine cheese
In a fuggy room

CHRISTMAS SEASON, 1817; OR "THE TIME MACHINE"

I stand at the controls now.
Others will have their turn, but this is mine.
It is the far future, you see, and all winds blow
Toward the path of memory.

I tell the machine to go back, to that night
We now call the *immortal dinner*;
And then go back a bit further,
To a dinner less remembered—

At the lodgings of Charles Lamb,
East India House clerk and essayist,
Where, like two stars in the December sky,
Wordsworth and Coleridge shine opposite!

Talking all the time, each one hath siphoned
His portion of the evening's guests.
This with wine, and that with brandy,
Each imbibed, for the bib was on his breast.

And I even see Crabb Robinson,
The thoughtful and impartial flaneur,
Moving between the far ends
Crowded of the splendid dining place.

I decide to join him—for I cannot be seen—
And together we race, like two planets
Between two stars, I make out of sync,
Whirling in blue convivial space.

Standing in the presence of Wordsworth
I downplay the dizzying whirl
Of visual impressions, and give my ear
Over to the stately rhythms of his verse.

I look at Crabb's face, transfixed
In the edge of the candlelight, which glows
And waxes in its breath-blown flickering,
And I can see him, listening.

And just as the cloud was beginning
To list and bounce its cloudy way
Reflected in the pristine waters of Windermere,
We're off tableside, bound for Coleridge Quay.

The long dark unexpected—as we fray
Out of that sphere of politic light.
Like a long tunnel, we cannot lose our way,
Except stopping to drink or take a bite.

I see him pause, and lift a piece of bread
To smear its face with pumpernickel jelly;
His mien is such, that I think he must
Need such ballast in his belly.

Smooth shores, and out of the shipping lane
We step, where wide before, in radiance is spread
The Commune of the Perfect Metaphor,
And I wish that I had had a piece of bread.

For here is the man I really came to see.
Coleridge, or what is left of him, recently gored
In the literary reviews, and far drunker
Than anyone suspects, especially his reviewers—

I spy Lamb amongst the growing crowd,

His blue-and-brown eyes twinkling in
The beauties of an irradiated recitation,
Thinking of that brash, and best lamentation

This century ever uttered for one of her own,
"An Arch angel a little damaged."
And it seems to me that he is watching Coleridge
"With steadfast eye"

"Among the choir of ever-enduring men"
"And as I rose, I found myself in prayer"
Coleridge reciting the verses of his Friend,
An Arch angel getting even.

But then we are off again—why, Crabb, why!
He turns a U around the table's end,
Pausing to touch a shoulder, to offer a smile,
And I smile alongside him, like a ghost;

And elsewhere, in Switzerland,
Shelley runs in terror from his post.
Back down the tunnel where I dread to walk,
For I fear at the exit, I will find my world waiting:

Soon we are climbing the ascent of Helvellyn,
I am struggling to keep up
With Crabb, who follows Wordsworth to the top.
I sit down and watch the sky, feeling clean-shaven

With every free-wheeling wind that carries by
The scent of a desolate sheepfold.
Halfway up the mount I turn my eye
Upon the world of shadows, far below.

Up on the peak, where the poet has climbed,
Even Crabb has balked and paused again

To rest within the confines of his shell;
In the distance, a low and solemn church-bell

Makes its low moan heard all across the distance,
And Wordsworth, in that famous stance
Of independence that we know so well,
Here turns his hawkish eyes in its direction—

For the first time that night, methinks,
He looks adown the slope to hear his Friend's
Long-forgotten question: why hast thou left me?
Still in some fond dream, revisit my sad heart!

Crabb takes longer beside the great table,
Just standing there unnoticed, loading food
Into his face. He is slowly unraveling.
The tides of time and force are pulling him apart.

In the midst of that seemingly infinite space,
I consider staying in between it all—
Here where it is Christmas, but a dark, sweet kind,
Silent, almost, as a suburb on a starry night.

But I'll not have him leaving me behind,
Lest I lose myself and never find my way
Back into the future. I try this time to grasp
A piece of bread, but my hand passes through.

Growing distractedly hungry, and thinking suddenly
That I have not smoked in some hours,
I fret at the edge of Coleridge's circle, while he frees
The mystery of human creative powers

From their small locked box within us all.
And a ghost that has haunted me up until now,
The ghost of Asra, summoned to his heel,

ADAMNEIKIRK

Stares long at me with a dispassionate brow.

FOR R. W. (1967 – 2009)

The Devil's greatest trick
Was convincing God
He was too wrathful.

I have a friend, a conman, who says
You were not pretty enough
For us to want to read you day after day.

You were no Sylvia Thoth, no Ann Sexpot.
You were actually better than them, he says.
Just unfortunately ugly.

He is proud to describe you as 'tough.'
Tough face. Thick skin. Yikes.
Mean mouth. Stiff lip, dark-haired.
You know, I heard she wrote some stuff.

As if that would save your legacy
From the invisible waters!
Making you hard and gritty, but clean.
As if one simply is, what they are said to be
(A critic's dream).

I have my suspicions. Every good poet
Wants to die, and knows a decent means.
The difficult thing is staying alive,
When death is such tough titty.

The truth is, for the living, you must own
Less worth than has
An abdicated throne.
And I must admit,

ADAMNEIKIRK

I no longer sharpen my wit
Against the smooth curve of your verse
When it hits. But it still hurts.

HARTLEY'S EXPOSTULATION / DERWENT'S REPLY

1.

I will not leave the Lakes on Saturday,
Not even to see a picture of the sky
Protrude a little over the hill and smile;
My home's among found village and lost way,
Just as my thoughts dwell elfly on the 'why'
Of all abandoned things—'tis that last mile
Out of the hinterland of childhood
Where you may find my footprints by the road
Full questioning and turning.

                         I have tried
To break predestiny with wild favor;
No measure of romantic feeling may
Free either one of us. When father died
Do you not feel that in us some dark pillar
Has turned forever, standing out of time?

2.

O, Hartley! You know—I have never understood
The creed in vatic verses; but that our foresight
Seems but a thing attached to elocution,
For this I love it, and suspect it lies.

You know, I have also never been a man
For shooting. You will not catch me, ever,
With a gun in my hand; or if you do,
It means the birds have long since flown.

I have always heard, however, that the mark
Of a true hunter is not the aiming straight,
But that he is quiet and still throughout and waits
For the perfect shot to find him in the dark.

O! a silliness; you see, in my case it has ever been
Enough, if I fix the hammer underneath my chin.

HOW MANY DROPS?

I did not know, when it began to rain,
And I with no hat, and no umbrella,
And a lecture-shirt, which recently de-stained,
Dearest Charlotte! in that fond libretto
Of groveling water, and by domestic strains,
Made picture-white, through effort of the brillo;
Where I should go, but, waylaid in a copse,
Never thy honor, but for thy innocence,
Stood and waited, awhile the viewless drops
Pelted on grove and bart, on lamp and fence,
And on the street, and on the red rooftops
All round me at irregular incidence.

And as I loitered there began to count
What silence grew between those pod impacts
To ask what silence properly amount,
Whether commenced on one, or end the next;
Or if indeed, through all that downward fount,
There be one moment not by water vexed!
Yet knowing, as I did, 'twas not a deluge,
But a spring shower: logic intervened,
And though I sought the dome of green's refuge,
I also vowed to stay until it weaned,
And tax my mathematic skill for you,
Dear Charlotte! for what comfort dryness mends.

MISTER ESTEESI

How can that lonely Albatross
Upon that wind its breath,
Suffice for the importance
Which attaches to its death?

In other news, self-questionings
Have never left the style;
Or am I honest all the time?
Or do I simply not realize

When I am telling lies?
Moreover, the result's the same;
It really should suffice.
To pull the wool over our eyes,

Must we count once beyond the first
Or count the first one, twice?

NOTEBOOK SPECULATIONS

The phenomenon of shaking the hand—
Physical touch of any kind, viz., an embrace,
The clapping on a shoulder, or when a man
Will sometimes, in first meeting, take
Another around the shoulders under his arm;
All gestures born out of the ancient instinct
To verify, that, yes, this other is real!
Of solid stuff, and will not disappear
The moment I have turned my back.

Compare to the way two lovers will
Hesitate by degrees between all touching;
It is as if the opposite were the case,
And that the one, I love, should vanish entire
The moment to espy their precious face.

ON 'THE BONDAGE OF LOVE'

"Coleridge was not suited, either by temperament or experience, to deal with the realities of this earth, neither in the guise of money matters ... nor in the shape of the emotional vicissitudes which are an integral part of day-to-day living ..."

Molly Lefebure, 1986

O cruel design of backward-glancing Age!
I throw the book to spite the offending page—
Judged by a woman of advancing years,
From me extracting crocodile's tears
I did not shed; torn from my marriage nest,
And made to lose again the battles lost.
Who are you, then, who have not sinned in living?
I pray you then, the Lord be more forgiving
That deep in time the holy death is buried.

'Tis one court who condemns the man unmarried,
Another wholly to condemn who has;
Still a third, come late, when he for wisdom tarried
In lands to part the purview of his spouse,
And make him seem a good man, who was not.
But what of woman's role, who does by rote
The making living, with the power of cribbing?
Judge her! To know a thing she has forgotten,
And take the trouble first to bring it up.

Now that Asra and I are in the grand sepulcher,
I am happy, and I commune daily
With the eternal truths my Reason once perceived;
But it does me wrong to read a page that waffles
'Twixt wisdom of its author, and the received

Opinion which thy troubled time dispense—;
Thou'rt fed and learned to feed inconstantly,
Half thought of me, and half disrupting sense,
That thou art made aggrieved, always, and already incensed.

POETICAL AUTOBIOGRAPHY

An amateur, who hit upon
An idle subject, drew him on
To other things which maybe weren't his business;

Like Angelond, in days of old,
Before the fires of faith grew cold,
And even ancienter days—practically mythic.

They stood out in his mind and soul,
For their green verdure, spread in full,
Along the banks of rivers which ran highly,

The whole Earth in a bloom of light,
The dim Earth, like an anchorite
Beshawled and looking on the Milky Isley.

Each star is like a fire far,
Each fire like a twinkling star,
Beyond that cloistered hovel where he lay;

And the night which blooms like an Earth-flower,
Improve the view with spectral power;
The spirits singing of the vanished day.

The slanted tombstones, in the yard
Beside the house where he was born,
Alas, that names and numbers now are faded;

To walk among them gravestones set
In the clayey soil near the parish step;
To walk along the river where they waded.

SOLITUDE

To show its worth to me I thought
To quote those ancient lines
Upon the lonely Yew-tree wrought
And written in the spines

Of books of poems, neatly-packed
Which Fancy nearly hallowed,
Bread crumbs upon the mental track
Imagination followed;

But how to show the dimpled page,
The corner bent, and fumbled?
The waiting on an empty stage,
The audience that grumbled?

He says to bring thee to the spot
Where an old man had vanished;
And where, of solitude begot,
The self, and duty tarnished,

To read some nameless in the wind,
To speak some wordless wonder,
To rest the body in the mind,
And hark the silent thunder.

And do you know that I have been
Almost to such fine places?
But picked out letters in the wind,
Of words their telltale traces,

And heard the storm you dread to hear,

Who thinkst, I hear it constant;
But listened without fright or fear,
Or regret for an instant.

Fain would I take thee with me, friend,
For all those tall strange meadows,
Those shadowed bowers, and misty bends,
Would make thy comforts settled,

That where I go, I've been before
In mind as well as spirit;
That madness is a mouse that roars,
If thou art deaf, to hear it.

STYLISH DOOM

I want to find some way
To bring together all the things I love
As in one room—& tethered by one soul
To be together in a stylish doom;
The world is ripe for something new and different
With echoes of the antient in its face.
The world is ripe for echoes—Hell, the world
Holds necessary arbors with an elf—
Invoking difference, invoking stirrings of war,
Empowering peace by ferocious display,
In a fanciful arena of green trees
Situated by a picture-perfect bay:
A room, deep in a house, by open water,
A gathering of friends from all over.

SYMPOSIUM

The rocks and trees bespeak a secret pain;
The landscape of your words, moves me with sadness;
Like a lake, frozen over with disdain:
Shadowy figurations under its surface.

But what indeed do they must figurate?
I've always wondered if the pain we feel
Is something localized that adumbrates
'Twixt light and dark, as shadows on a field,

And finds a way to hide, and a way to speak;
Or if it something more, a mystery of being
Surpassing body's bounds and mind's foggy break—
Ere-growing and oblique—requiring special seeing.

Perhaps the poet is in love with death
Precisely wrong, that it is like this problem—
We feel that when we die, must our soul's breath
Depart most through expansion and enlargement,

And run away from us, at last away.
And love—in her best form, a quiet salve—
Which in her passion wounds the burn, and slays
The ill, and shouts us into life alive—

Too seems a second self, which grows beyond
This dreary inch of life, which we have worked for.
So he would like to die well out of love,
Give away his mind to the world, and dream no more.

But there in ignorance we have got him.

For in his going wrong, he but betrays
Something of the path which lies hidden,
Missed by inches on his life's long way.

That what we seek, is like an anti-body,
And does not need to think, so it has no mind;
How oft in history did we embody
As Death a quality of death in kind.

But now that for some dying seems so far,
Pushed ever anon by white technologies,
What else on earth resemble this fond other?
How do we read the sadness of the trees?

THE DEAD

I feel the dead holding my hand;
They hold me in their distant land.
How soft their ribbons, how rotted curls,
And the sense of a wail that whirls and swirls;
Shall comfort me when, by God's plan,
I must awake, and live as man.

THE EXPERT

Is it a wasted opportunity
Not to write a poem now
When I am listening
To a song that I longed to hear?
And feeling my expertise
Which is the expertise
Of the poet
Do its difficult stride of power?

Strength strongs;
And quickness darts along—
The intellectual waits
Upon the beauty of a soft verdict.
The sensuous abound
In all things great and small;
But the expertise of poetry
Is simply, not to fail.

We must share so much
Of our secret world
With others,
That it must lose
To every prying eye
Its quality of secrecy;

It must become
Something we pass away from
In our neediest hour
When we seek
Silence and solitude.

The expert poet waves his wand
Slowly and with great internal pain
Along the horizon of that world—
Making everything simpler, brighter,
Less wonderful than it was—

It is impossible for him to work
And not install the gaudy fixtures
Of a certain kind of showmanship.

So then, the young, who are
Creatures of darkness
Who long to write their souls
Who stare out of the dim places
Hungry and forlorn
Like forest creatures

Complain that he is
A kind of traitor to his kind,
Ambushing the old haunts
With streaming sunlight.

Do you think I can install a star?
Even I cannot do that.
I only remind the Sun, a little
More light this way, thank you.

But that he must oblige us,
With his great face and head
Peeking in on our little, lovely places—

You must accept this as a fact of life.

THE HEDGE WITCH

If I have something troubles me,
'Tis best I keep it to myself;
If I have something that troubles me,
I durst not write it down in verse,
That makes the human passions free,
If I have something that troubles me.

I best not break a line to let
The mind's reflections turn to that
Something that troubles me; nor end
The stanza once begun: for such, unspake
Might make reflection pause and see,
If I have something troubles me.

To go on there, 'twould quote the danger;
'Tis best to remain, myself, a stranger.
Nor know myself, nor any other,
Though might my sister or my brother;
If I have something troubling me,
Why tell a thing that can't, for them,
Be felt, but in its infancy?
If I have something troubling me.

THE LAST DAYS OF A MAGICIAN [FRAGMENT]

I.

I feel a loss, a deep within my soul
On winter tracks; in gardens not my own;
Or strolling slowly by the River Colne
I sigh and give in, firm without control.
Spring is coming, but the sky is long
With narrow clouds like ribbots in a dyer;
The things of joy, and double things of ire
Make plenty of sound – but sound is not song –
I listen without pleasure or desire.
A sound more near to me, a smattering sound,
An under-sound is with me all along
Not where the tender reed up from the ground
Beneath the water grows; but a fit pond
Down where I think about the sound of water.

II.

The excalibur, rising with a drop
Of obsequious Merlins, shines with Arthurian light.
The Merlins dance upon the hilt and blade
With baldly motions in a mistlike glade,
The Christmas starlings wheel in happy flight,
The year has almost come to a full stop.
The ancient utters, the palm at my side,
The priestly robes which I forebore to don,
Make morals which my phrases just elide;

I seem to walk among the shadows of fun.
The earth is full of loss and its rich hide
Conceals from us the judgments of the dead;
The atmosphere is light; inside of my head
I dream of Heaven young and alive at night.

III.

O Gibley Woods, or Chumney, or St Bastion's Rood,
O warrowing circle of a dim-made road;
This worst, this plan, and boar upon the track,
This over growing, we cannot release;
Adept with progress, we cannot take back,
And servant to high men whom we cannot please,
Hath made me pensive in a random wood,
As sly and watchful as an anytoad;
With my shut fat eyes and my spring-making hollow
I sat on a squat rat in the Minster's Hollow,
My eyes the tongues of nervous flies to follow,
And speaking when its silence would allow,
Made a mouth with rang with words of a proud town,
A prosperous city, and a nation with an ugly frown.

IV.

From the capital city doors and windows would be
Open at all hours allowing voices
To carry news between stations; the tardy laborer
Could hear the day's events upon the paving road
Being ticked down great and green in their dearth of true
Newsworthy material; the long lists of famed
Names, who like a cycle of minstrel's air
Travel from here and there in a friendly circle
Might charm in part the laborer with delight

To dream of music, art and the spoken word
Touching the basins of his children, fair
Trade plied willingly between free citizens
From the top of the motel window to the street
A sprinkle of dreams on the grey foam of sleep.

THE SPIRIT OF REASON

An idea had come to him, an idea fresh,
One lazy afternoon in Cambridge town,
As he lay disposed upon a chaise longue.
That all the world might be, for all we knew,
Like that scene which drew his eye
Beyond the window:

      The painted look of bodies passing by,
When they were still, for just a moment, to stare in
The facing glass of shopfronts, the display
Of wares for purchase, fineries beyond
The reach of means, but not the reach of mind.

A woman underneath a parasol,
Admiring a Parisian parasol;
The shadow of coolness on her brow, to see,
Its symmetries, like buttresses, and its filigree.

Her eyes frozen in regard: he could almost spy
The up-down motions of her heart behind,
A child straddled on a busy bellows.
The breath drawn in, to strain the hidden corset,
And the gloved hand tightening over the rod,
The lips fair tightening, too, beseeching God.

The Reason leaving, like a flume of smoke,
The body's grossness, which the corset choked,
The Spirit of Reason was a sapphire ghost
Oblivious to the light-falling rain.

Another man, far younger, almost swayed

Where he stood underneath the Butcher's sign,
The limbs and appendages floating out like gas,
Smelling foreign *venison*. The head, inclined
Far back to curry the scent; which hurried past
To tempt the Spirit that had not been caught.

On down the street, a child shivering with cold
Watched the fishmonger with his brawny arms
Upraise the cleaver quick and carry it out
Upon the silvered bodies of the fish,

His stand and feet, heavy-booted, carved out
By heavy blocks of ice. All afternoon,
He watched the child watch the pale gray fish,
Round eyes staring up in perfect circles.

In his future, a thing unknown to him
As a stranger hidden in a crimson curtain,
His likeness would be captured in a painting
Bleared, but recognizable, by time,
By long waiting, and by the many secrets
Of love, and false belonging. Here in this work,
Behind the image of the great man,
Just behind his sad moon-like face,
Floating here and there in the portrait's dark,
Soft shimmers of sapphire ghosts, all one,
Broken apart in their restlessness,
Like a woodland stream divided into channels
When it begins to feed a cultivated ground.

THROUGH THE LAYERS OF FOUNDATION & THE BEAUTY-MARK

Over all; the image of the eighteenth-century
Poseur, with his garden of ruined towers—
Like an infinite series of dramatis personae,
Dramatic, non-humanity: turning away,
Throwing one arm across the weeping face;
Together with his beloved in the small white
Vine-encrusted flower-sporting gazebo
Twisting like two entwining spirits; the great
Moon overhead where the mist has all been spread,
The old enchanted wood shot through with moon,
The gently lilting sound of the pianoforte.

It has been a long time since my darling Muse
Was not, herself, one of these series gothique;
Disguised at last by the bits and pieces of
Ironic historical knowledge for the amuse-bouche,
Barely to view, her gold and smiling face
Through the layers of foundation and the beauty-mark;
To walk with the perfect grace of a dancer
For a few steps at a time; or a lantern which,
Being turned slowly and rotated in the hand,
Gives out sweet light its first two pristine lenses,
Diffuses it in latter lenses with filthy lack of pretense.

You know, we tried everything to fix the light,
Even downgraded to a weak bulb or to a flame,
Anything for a constant light, to set a constant mood,

Even if the place was hardly seeable!
But this is not a problem which we can repair
From the outside, or which can be cosmetized somehow;
If you have derived a kind of best bet approach—
And I know you have, for that is what you do—
You will have to put it into practice in secret,
And if it is somehow successful, well, this is the hard part,
You will have to enjoy that success in alternate reality.

TO MY STUDENTS

Westfield State University
2017-2019

I teach them in the dark
While great winds roar

And a wide dismal sound
Surrounds us: a furor

Of notions, mostly impossible;
And also, the great, lumbering,

Disassembling steps
Of giant-eyed History,

Shaping the unseen earth
And making the sky shiver.

Though it is dry
Within this bone-white cupola

My words drown
In a torrent of their own:

Thought, remark, and flip aside,
Fill up pneumatic bodies;

And they, like children
With lunatic minds,

Do not realize how tightly
They have enclosed their souls.

They do not know
They wear smiles of false welcome.

Not one drop of the World
Shall enter, who is not ready.

Instead, we seem to practice
The moment they will lose

Their sense of fear. What
Will they ever replace it with?

"UNDOUBTEDLY"

The young Ambitious
In the drawing-room

The large eyes like two
Craters staring

Into the Sun;
The roguish locks

Which lay
With unkempt purpose;

The torrent flow
Of imparsible speech

Inseparate topics
Unfecundly white and new;

The True, The Good
And how the moon

Foretells a coming storm;
The blue

Invisible energy
Tendrillic and spindly

Painting
The cold hillside

With trees which
Sprang from the soil,

ADAMNEIKIRK

Full-grown and with
Their blossoms shed already

UTOPIA

For Granny and Sheryl

So much of life
Is sitting and waiting and thinking about
The smell of tobacco on your grandfather's nose

The driveway made up mostly of white stone,
The roots of trees interacting with it all,

Ivy-trellised walls, a dangerous road,
A black iron archway leading us toward

Chinese candles hung about
The red wraparound porch and
Broken wicker chaise lounges whose

Busted pillows spill their meaningful dust
Across a poem printed on a tea towel
Clayed and wattled in the recent past;

Moldering wasp-ridden yurts, where sat
The sickbeds of French diplomats

The huge unslicked stones' pressed notions
In soil and the crossing yellow bridge that

Atop the edges of homebuilt ponds defeats
Selfish fish who don't fly, but still meet
In the ecclesiastical waters' shallow seat;

Garlic garden, slim white picket fence,

He always tended, and asparagus

In shadows of early summer and Thanksgiving
Atop the rows of the holy fishbones
Picked cleanly from the bodies' silver lining;

The huge room, on the thirdmost floor, with outré books;
Faded maps of the centers of industry
Blocking the holes in the roof

Yawning abysses, light dawn
At the edges of sleep

Where
Posters and disregarded lecture notes
And a huge red down-filled coat
Make nests for bats to piss in private nooks.

The trapdoor hidden
Behind the moving bookcases which held
A gift box of pewter knights and samurai;

Berserkers with their masks of rage;
And the woman who died
To protect it all

Big fluffy basketball
Inside a white pine forest—

Taking breaths like one has goes against
A carnival game: alert, unconvinced

The soft ragbags of the spirit now,
Which one had torn like gobs of flesh back then,
Tossed like knotholes through the blessing of sin;

And the walking dead casked away in a wine cellar,

Faulknerian drunks
Lying in rivers of gold!

The house, I want to tell her, is a ghost,
A monster untouched by public discourse;

A place too lavish to keep up, if it
Does not contain, first, the blessing of the perished
And secondly, a new layer of paint

The red and black, amphidamee
And oriental room
Rug's cigar-black craters

The famous French sword that slew
The German dragon Humperdincht;

And thirty thousand porcelain Santa Claus hummels
Together in congress on a white oak table

Before the statue of Buddha,
With the shadow of Jesus' pity lain
Like stubble on the laughing face

One kneels in the sandals of originality

Like caterpillars
We do not breathe

And have exhausted ways to say we need
A break or do-over, a new start

But deep and inland there is a sweet-dream sea,
Further than you can remember it—it puckers the air

With its expansive breaths, and makes a cloak
A cove and a secret lake like Derwent Water
At the bottom of her duck-laden farmer's slope

Nearby the town of Keswick stands
On its hands outside of a breakfast café,
Walking her dogs in the twilit park

And the boats which launch from the jetties at the end
Of summer fly to Hawse in green-toed mist;

Lying together with you in the dark
Of misremembered bliss

I wonder if we will ever make it back
To the places I was grown, and formed, and kissed

YOUR LITTLE HEART

A faint half-love surrounds my tepid heart—
A little wrapping sail of font and flow;
It reaches out—as with a child's arms—
Reaching for something that it cannot know.
But that it reaches out, it reaches all
Discriminates no type of what it draws
To itself in its embrace; it pulls the world
With coyness and a hesitant guffaw
A little closer to its downcast face,
Then sidles partway with a shuffle-step,
Muttering on some secret or another;
But to think on what that meant to it:
That passion is another word for smother!
Then peeks so shyly at the all of all,
And loves, in silence, what is loud and drawn,
With small and quiet words that lead the band
Of raucous flowers, when they laugh at dawn—

Or seeking breaths that shelter in the wind;
O'er the million stars that hide behind the sun;
The moon's fond favor when she looks on him—
Just squeezes all the many into one.
It makes a heart of what is not, and finds
The sound of heartbeats in what makes no sound,
Wrapped in the sailcloth of a freaking atom,
Or scattered in the air, and over the ground.
And here it finds its lunch and sustenance,
And holds it all in continuity—;
The fleck and flavor needs no livery—

It holds it all in perpetuity—
For all of air, and sea, and sky, and white,
The arms of dazzle through the bird-blown blue,
And the arms of spirals in the sky at night,
It spreads to capture, infinite and true.

But let that not end here our fond heart's tale;
She runs the gamut from the zinc to aqua;
And lives again in blended words, and operas,
And like her heroes loves the greenly dale.
No abber-spabber spasterisk can tame her;
Nor linguid lango pause that steam which fires
Out of her veins and fuming arterires;
Her light shines through the errors which would blame her—
Her song is heard behind the glorious choirs
Of men and angels, and the demons roaring.
Her dream is in the roughs of old men snoring,
And she is broken like the strings of lyres
Upon the rocky world-stage of the world,
And bashed to pieces for her many sutures.
Nor is she food again for scheming vultures,
Misgendered, and from steeply ramparts hurled;
But stains herself upon the coifs of virgins,
And bleeds her vigor on the temple girls.

No let me try and yes I will avert her,
Who lives and whispers nonsense that I make
Into half-senses that will tease the thinker—
That happy nonsense Zarathustra spake!
The world is links, and gleeful is the linker;
His fingers hurt from bending all the day;
As if to write—and write with joy to mend her—
Were bone for sake of metal chain to break.

Now let the happy heart resume its silence,
And hide again behind its wind-torn door;
God bless me with a blessing to remember,
I'll think of *leeches* on the lonely moor!
Or lie in somnolence in sisty verdas,
I sum the liver, and I sweeten the eye;
I once walked up the height to see the glory,
And slipped, and fell back down the other side.
But it's alright—it's alright—it's autumnal,
With winter breaking in the branches green;
Or did you see the colors of that April?
The pescatary bauble of the stream.
The slip and fall, and rise again in silence,
The utter cumbrous wondertude of yore,
The display of something more than wit and license,
Running on and chattering on for

IV: IPSWICH

2022—2023

ANIMA

Death shines like a light
That is brighter than light
From the edge of the black
Dark chamber of night

In the back of the room
Of the womb of the soul
Through a little round space
In a little round hole

Where my eye seems to stick
When I'm sad or I'm sick
Or I can't catch a break
And my brain is a wreck

Then I stare at the light
With my eye on the key
Like a star in the night
Floating happy and free

But I don't make a wish
For it is not a star
And it isn't so bright
And it isn't so far

Death shines like a light
From the edge of the black
That is brighter than light—
What's brighter than that?

ARIGHT

Every year that passes,
Another person we don't know
Lays in the silent tresses
Of the winter's pathless snow;
Another lights a lamp, who fain would view
The shape of lambent shadows stress the hue
Of the frosted hedge-row;
Another cups the match against the wick,
Willing the sulfur brighten.
Now, I don't mean to frighten you
But the next time you are sick could be your last.
Who, in the past, will arrange the parade of when,

As you have passed, their forces clump together,
One friend to palm the matchstick, one to shiver
A bulwark to the wind? Don't let it be blown out
By icy fiends with cackling zero mouths,
The light from which your shadow seems to flee:
Who will open the tome, the drawer, the suitcase,
Finding your Christmas letters, your stuffy old clothes?
Who conduct procession from the pews?
And who hang up the candle of your nose,
Squinting to see the seashore where, like Friedrich's monk,
You struggle to remember your own face?
Who yet will exasperated grow? Saying "enough is enough"?

CELEBRATING MY PH.D. AS A DIABETIC

I promised my wife I wouldn't smoke
And I haven't drank since I got nasty
With her at an academic conference
Last year, so instead I eat an ice cream cone
That I know is slowly killing me,
Enjoying it as eagerly as a child
While trying, as always, to savor every bite.
It's really the problem of death
And the fact that my achievement is meaningless
In the wider world that should occupy me,
Not my inability to properly savor
An ice cream; but if I can't even do this,
If I can't, for example, realize
That she is my best reader,
That she knows more than she says,
That she lets me talk—and talk—about myself—
My problems—my fixations—my bad
Publication record—my transparent genius—
Even late into the night, when she is sleepy?

CELESTE

Is it normal to cry for no reason?
No one has ever asked that; Reason is Just,
Time is Forthright. In the pocket of your corduroy pants
There is an out-of-season fruit,
Waiting for your mouth. Don't let it win.

Unhand me, blackguard rogue! I have spent for a year
Straining to adjust this long grey glove,
Standing quietly in a room by myself,
Listening to the sounds from outside.

No sound has reached me into this mind-mix experiment.
I am tuckered out. I jive and pulse
Although I cannot strobe; I confess to the
Parental nebulae that I have failed them.
They glimmer back, coo-coo baby stars;

And all at once, the long night, like a player piano scroll,
Rolls down into the earth—and a giant music
"Dances and sings" an old man on a rag-stick—
"We have been waiting for you! And we have not yet seen you!"

Ah, so what. This glimdimmery vale
Seizes me in the same rapture as an office building.
The unfolded night, so gentle to behold,
Triggers a panic attack when it comes in
To my dreams. The lights in my flat all go out,

ADAMNEIKIRK

There is a feeling of menace, and then I awaken.

DEATH AND TAXIDERMY

For Papa Stoney

It isn't anyone's fault, really, that the world happens to conspire
And take our love for granted, and renege
Its few sweet gifts. With a bit of wire

And some stuffing of our mind's own management,
We falsify the insides of what's left,
Make something whole that is not really there

Fill up the room that was just laid bare,
And anchor lay, by bit, old sofa, misshapen chair,
A window, with an empty place

Upon the sill which never once refused
A foot, the pane that stills your phantom face.
Materials you left can be reused,

And dregs you failed to drink can still be drank,
But the world you built now shrinks around, and like with mine has shrank.

EATING DESSERT

How can you make that scrap of clothing
Cover your entire body
Or that patchy sleeping-bag
Into a temple of Nyx
Or that patchy beard
Like a black carpet to the ceremony
In which you are crowned, coronated
By a single piece of gold?
A single person stands before you,
Representing, by divine transfluence,
The entire population

A single kiss on the hand, a meaningful look,
Holding your hand a long time by the fire,
Behind her back, a compliment well-paid,
A single grain of rice, a power nap of 20 minutes or less

These are all just examples
We're not even in outer space yet
This is just the beginning, I say
Sharpening my knives on the knife-wheel
We have come so far
With so little left to go on
You, I and her
Getting our jollies doing this, doing it well sometimes

Is love
Making the most of barely anything
Or the know-it-all man (love is an uncle)

Saying, with self-conscious pleasure,
Ah, but it is *something rather than nothing*

GHOSTLY GROVE

After Stephen Sexton

Sometimes the rope we thought we were climbing and getting to somewhere
Disappears while we are still holding onto it and then we fall.
An interlude begins in our life, one that doesn't remember
The sound of laughter wooshing through the air, the way it felt when we
Had the whole world spread out beneath us. It was the ghosts the whole time.
Instead, here we are, standing in the woods as if we'd always been
Meant to look and listen only so we can catch the next wind.

GRIEF

Grief!
Grief makes you pepper butter in the sink
Instead of the knife you spread it on.
Makes your brain do
Funny things. Read things twice.

Second guess yourself. Like, *Do I have
Generalized anxiety disorder?* Suddenly the grief you feel
With your finger on the button, prepping to express,
Is undeniable. You stand in pause beside the telephone.

Grief finishes you for sport.
Not just your whole ass, but the flesh of you remaining
Goes in paper form into the belly of grief.

I LOVE TO WATCH YOUR SLEEPING FACE

I love to watch your sleeping face
Lying in gentle repose,
All those lines—of smiling, laughing
Crying and frowning—have departed

Leaving only your nose
Perched on top of your mouth
Like a poor tradesman,
Benighted, considering his options

His horses ran off
In the moonlight's glow
And the surrounding woodlands crawl
With prowling bandits

Now he sits, a little slumped
Beside a slow-moving stream,
Thinking of tomorrow's riches

IN ENGLAND

The way she'll point out a landscape
I've already seen
A loose mixture, like so many things
In England and on Earth
Of growing industry
And the green of distant fields

The dust on a busy road
Sprinkled here and there
With the dust of whimsical pixies
Saying, 'Ooh!'
Excitedly she knows
I am looking at her

The way she'll hand me water
In a bullet-shaped bottle
Above the table of our train,
Nervously glancing
To see if I am drinking enough
Or too much

She plays with her hair
That was recently cut short
Falling messily to her shoulders
Twisting up her face
She becomes lost
In her smartphone again

I never long to read her thoughts
While I am staring vacantly

From the window
At a rolling landscape,
Waiting patiently for
The future to arrive

Or when I see her
Quietly downturned face
Her eyebrows rising and falling
Like hot-air balloons
In the cloudless heaven
Of this willowy world

Yet there is some part of me
Some distant part,
Ancient, but perhaps still
Close at hand that wonders
If our souls can touch
Through the unspent years

If choosing a life together means
That in some transcendent space
We are grafted together
Like two old trees
Whose roots and boughs
Have become entangled

If beneath us
In the gold of universality
Industry and beauty-free
A child rests in the brief shade
We make with our bodies,
Or longer in our soul shadows

JOB

you can't get one
the world, behind a curtain, seems
to say; it wouldn't be fair
to the thousands of others
for whom each day is a slow-pitched
grey ball with dark blue stitches.
September is the month of school

each calendar month is a color
and this one is faded paper,
red and blue lines inside
a blue book with a blank space
and your name not yet written
floating in a desk's gum-covered armor

and it wouldn't be fair
to the millions or billions
who are no longer with us,
who were born and who died
in an age of long hours,
likelihood, gainful, meaningful
light on a shop's front window

it isn't your job
to get free of this
or return to the past.

LAYING UNDER THE CHRISTMAS TREE

These profound feelings travel in your blood,
And make you sentimental; so you brood
Laying beneath the decorated tree
Your eyes on all that Christian Christmas food.

Thoughts like, "The five (or six?) Romantic poets were
Like demons to their age, although in ours
Are now like Saints, whom we cannot escape,"
Dominate your mood, your waking hours.

So I 'remembered' you – you came to me
A second or a third time in your way,
Appearing like a phantom in my dreams,
Apposite of some game board that you played.

And by a codex of your own design,
Which took me, like a sentimental man
Who wrests with knowledge, ages to unwind,
You made it clear why we cannot be friends.

These are two different stories. Who but Coleridge
Could analyze where they begin and end?
Who but Shelley, standing on Mont Blanc,
Discern two nations destined for awards?

The fact is, we are friends, and we were friends.
You haven't spoken to me for many years.
I don't know where the tales begin and end.

But I can see that mountain through my tears.

LUIGI

It is only beside Mario that he is tall.
And yet, he is taller.
And it is only beside Mario that he
Is thin. And yet, thinner he is.
He, Luigi, is the Mario Brother
Whom we can most relate to—
Because he is afraid of ghosts.
Because he wants "to be a great plumber
Like his brother, Mario"
(He says this so we'll leave him alone).
Because he inherited
A sprawling, haunted mansion
That he knows not what to do with.
Even when the frights and fractured feelings
Free him from his self-imposed green shell,
It is only with a shaking hand he harries
Reluctantly fell fiends of Koopadom,
Or like brave Dante journeys into hell,
A massive salmon struggling through the fire.

He dreams, like many, the day that he'll retire—
Big-toed feet propped on the wicker swell,
A cold one in his hand, and to the waves
Which on the backs of other waves their tongues
In silence slosh or lash, the de-tongued bell,
He listens, with a frisson free and clear.
Darkly as in some corner of his mind
A rounder with a blush her face reverts;
When he is resting, and his singing hurts,

He cups a surfboard underneath his arm,
He holds it like his own he used to fear,
Own now it is not his to keep from harm,
He holds for that reason ever more dear.

MILKWEED

Waking up beside the river of my dreams
I want to set off again
Into this frozen forest
That surrounds this little town
Where Bluebell has carried me

We must risk something, always
I once wrote, in a turgid letter
To a former friend

He later said (or quipped)
How is anyone supposed to respond to that?

The idylls, which seem
To be locked away in lostness,
In the getting lost, or the letting go

The power of the individual
Courting his freedom in an unknown land
Won't you join me?

I have led my horse this far,
Holding her by the reigns
Near the settled snow

In the distance, there is a sound like
A tinkling sound I read about once—

Between frozen trees,
Threatening where the bark has split

To explode (comma),

The air is so thin, so pure—
The eye delights to sting and pawn its tear
On the nearest sympathizer (comma),

The human objects, you know the soft ones,
Who stand between these trees,
Feeling threatened, feeling transported

Waiting to feel something,
They last forever in that moment
Before

Attuning their minds to language, and the mire
Of the unorganized, they pause, they expect
They wait, and have I mentioned

The way the heart beats
When the body is wounded
When all the flesh is frozen through

The way that blood flows
When it has nowhere to go?
Or the et ceteras that make us crazy (comma)

Just outside of the town,
Passing, unheard of, through the guard-like gates
The open world, the sense of danger
The ability which we have honed for half our life
Getting the better of us

NYANG

Today was a weird day. A day of shifts, strangles,
And exhortations, but a day
On which neither of us said very much.
A day on which I thought I had
The feeling that we might be standing
At the end of a long, interminable bridge
Dangling over a precipitous canyon.
But we live beside the marina, in a squat square
Building where the sun often shines in:
A fifth-floor waterfront flat.

While jetties go, sunbathed and moss-kissed,
Off toward unknown water, we have never
Been allowed to set foot upon them.
We walk upon the oceanic footpath,
Past coffee shops, old disused buildings, street art.
In the middle distance, yachts
Bob and sway like the lights of a circus.
They have names like *Kea Two*,
Gloria Albion and *Nyang*.
They come from all over the world,
Gathered here in silent congregation
While summer fades into—not fall—
But some other thing.

Sometimes we watch them slowly
Making to sail, heading out
To the Atlantic ocean, or to France;
And once, we saw a man

And his wife struggling to keep one
From floating away.

OLD BLUEBELL

Shaking the reigns in the falling snow,
I'm reminded of the time we went for Starbucks
Coming back from M&S to buy Christmas snacks
Ahead of our visit to Wilko

To buy you nasal spray;
The empty street, which led into
That cavernous hollow
Somehow fled from day

And the way the silver cups
Were tiered, and the syrup bottles empty,
The flavorings, and the gallon milks, all empty,
Gone out to the world's endless sup

Feeding the semi-busyness of people.
Variety and caffeinated soup
Accompanied us on our flat-town-flat loop,
And we walked beneath three pretty amazing steeples.

Now I am alone, except for old Bluebell
Gnawing companionably at her bridle.
These lazy flakes fall down, and I am idle,
Reflecting how it is a kind of hell

To be a lonely rider in the night,
The soundless night, except a distant bell
From Sanctuary is pealing out its knell,
And there isn't a Starbucks in sight.

PLEASE CAN YOU REMOVE ME FROM THIS MAILING LIST

Please can you remove me from this mailing list
Me too

I subscribed while I was a PhD student
Me too please

When ongoing industrial actions across the university
Me too x
Seemed more pertinent

Now that I have been awarded my doctorate
And lost access to my university email
Me as well thanks
And all other IT services

And me
And I am waiting to hear back
From potential jobs and postdocs
Me too please

I find the constant deluge of university-related
Me too
Jargon-infused emails
And me thanks x
Rather distracting

Please stop hitting 'reply all' to ask to be unsubscribed

It takes two clicks to unsubscribe through IT portal

ADAMNEIKIRK

And slightly painful to read
Now can we get back to the matter at hand?
If you can understand what I mean

PROLOGUE

This plague-war between Alsoor and Ghed
Has left me on my head:
Traveling south to escape the cold grippe,
Not like Old Jodah, a sword on his hip,
A fire in his heart, and magic in his hands
Drawn forth from memories of peaceful lands;
I have fled away. And running now remark,
"My, how faithfully the shadowing dark
Diminishes into the north! I have seen yet
White flowers beautiful and wet
Spring up beside bald rushes in the sun,
Where'er the gentle river runs,
And listened further, to the purple gloom,
Far from the precipice of doom,
Birds sing their dream-arranging songs
With melodies both short and long
That dance along the forking olive tree."

That is my fate. While Jodah he
Turns north, to find his master languishing,
And friend and foe alike go anguishing
Around him, in the claws of horror-tide,
I do not live as with an ice inside;
I sing, I melt a bit, and southward turn
While he (and those like him) have all the fun.
And while he is assuredly right—
And follows Vorsk, and the burning spell-light—
I will go south, and save my life,
And tell of all, whatever joy or strife

ADAMNEIKIRK

That happened there, I can recall.

PUFFY HAT

it is necessary to begin again
the world doesn't have your best interests at heart
and other platitudes never occurred to me;
the predictable pause between saying
'I'm sorry' 'I know it's wrong' or 'I wish
there was something more to be done'
doesn't happen in the shower
because the smaller the room
the slower the sense of returning

there is no great loss in not getting to wear
a doctor's bonnet; in the photos we paid for
when the young professional photographer
directed the angle of my chin, the height
of my shoulders, and you stood in
beside me as I clutched the brick-red
parchment case, the puffy hat
could have also been on your head

who is going to remember?

and indeed, one expansively
surmises the puffy hat could still appear
on the head of an unbeliever, on a non-
scientist, or even an anti-intellectual,
it could even appear sort of on its own
masking the horizon like a puff of smoke
or a whiff of something visible,
standing in a glade of late-day shadows

ADAMNEIKIRK

with nobody around to admire it

RAMONA

Sometime last night
You were wung into the world
Wrapped up tight
In a bundle of curls
A Christmas baby
That we wanted to visit
For reasons that
We shan't revisit,
We couldn't make it
I had tried
Don't worry, I'll make it
Another time

I hope I'm there now
When you read this poem
I wrote for you
But if I'm not
Try to remember
The good first stanza
And forget about this one

I already forgot
My own birth, you know
Most people do
But we have photos of you
And your mother, Amanda
Lying together
On a bed of dreams
And maybes

I look at your face
Searching for family resemblance,
Living my best life
As I stare into my phone
In a darkened English room

You will learn to count squares,
Dot I's, and reassemble willows;
Sometime there won't be a better friend
Than your pillows;
I made a joke about you becoming
A Jedi or a Sith—
Will you give the world a hug,
Or a kiss?
See, poems are easy
Just write what you think
Then make it sound pretty
With assonant links
I sure hope you, baby
Will see me sometime
I probably live there
On somebody's mind

The day is starting and we
Are another person richer,
Another person poorer. I hope
You think about that
You will acquire the world
But also, it will acquire you
And if someone hasn't told you lately
There are some who will say
God bless you
Whenever you sneeze

Or fall on hard times

But there are some who will say
God bless you
For no reason,
Like right now

There's no time or space
When life is at its best

There's no end of difficult things also
It's like a test

There's no end of infinite spirits which dwell
Inside of us all
Like clear-water wells

There's no end of waiting
But you're finally here!
Have a Merry Christmas, baby
And a Happy New Year

SUDDENLY

Who knows how somesuch thing can multiply,
Or how an unparticular thing can end?
While he is smoking, while boats are passing by
On the wakefield of pure terror, water as glass
I am leaving the fourth grade and passing through
The hole in the silver and deep green great grey fence:

While he is smoking, and the woman in his teeth
Has got up her pale and shovel, the old,
Withered, deep-eyed nurse hath raised
Her ancient and slender hand and now withdraws
A little gavel from her white smoke coat:
DING she pounds it on the storeshop bell—

I find myself, against all accounting of sense,
At the front of the queue, shaking like a leaf,
With perfect solicitousness and solitude.
I amble forward, hands stuffed in the pockets
Of my brown, incredibly strained, skin-hugging trousers,
In my ripped up, purple, wine-like remnant shirt,
So large and well-defined, that I may well
Be naked in this green beyond the grey
Where I still am?

Then she asks me for my name, but before
(I can see it in her gaze which threats
To pull the vigor from my heaving breast)
I give her that, I have to show that I
Am really the owner of the number she

Hath called out in her pealing creak-bell voice.

While I am doing this, she is looking directly
Into my eyes; imagine, reader, her well-seasoned eyes
Smartly beneath the brim of a white cap.

Her sea-like flesh, and the wrinkles like brown dunes,
And her mouth, a strangle not yet verified,
Presides around her face like a Shadow-Pope,
Curved off a little to the side and down,
A kind of autotransmitted smirk, which now
Assumes its opposite without intention:
Like a lonely lover while the sun is going down,
He smiles at the dark without resentment;
Lips of black cherry, both a penny, and a nickel,
And a cigarette from nowhere, and a young town
On the coast of a crumbling island empire;
While I am trying to gather up my strength,
Me huge hulk of a drifter, who has been
A thousand times to the front of this line,
The millions of souls behind me yet stretch back
And hit the backmost wall and start to stack.

TAKE MY CAR

I don't know who you are.
And I don't know what this Tweet says—it's in Japanese.
But I know that, for the moment, your car
Is filled with snow. How will you get home?

Take mine. It glides. And on it we'll glide home,
Through frosty streets, through river's abandoned town,
Over the lights of defunct shopping malls,
And the colder abbeys of steel mills, rented out
To haberdashers; salty, venomous merchants
With their feet plant in two worlds
Huck snowballs at us gliding as we pass
With our feet stanched to oblivion. They won't last.

Humphrey, Digbert, and Luminous Billy, your array
Of stuffed animals won't live another day
In that old shitbox; give them a ride in mine,
And they'll grow organs, thoughts of human worth,
And become real—I promise you. In time
They will decamp those long and endless fields
With pop-up tents and shabby stalls their own,
And grow their network of economy;
And one will blast, and one will turn to Jesus,
And one live on old cheese, and one compose symphonies
In motor oil under a failing bridge. They'll do all this
As we did, but replace
The squinting faces of the angry mob
That gathers in my soft tires' traceless tracks,
And the smoke of my exhaust in memory.

TEEN GOHAN

I cannot tell you what he must have felt—
In that moment, famous to us now
In memory and reality,
That moment made so famous years before
In which, one losing everything, one gains
In the first passage of a thin-made dream
His father's relocations—Namek, Yardrat,
Vegeta and Otherworld, Heaven, Hell, and the Lilliputian
Kai Planet;

          To do it twice, like,
To have done it once before; when justice overloads
This human-seeming body, and suddenly
Everything which had threatened us
Is no more.
This is the fantasy of millions.

To force the unripe flower into the light
Of a sun which burns from within. What would
Happen to the skin? The eyes—would they change?
The hair? The hair! The scholar's glasses broken in half,
The worldly ledger unraveled like an endless snake,
The weekend girlfriend taken the weekend off,
While your mother worries, cries and squirms
Over a broken television set. The helicopter blades
Beat the supercharged air. *This is ZTV.* And the perfectly sculpted face
Of a monster is suddenly puffy, bald, inhuman—but fair
—

Only you still struggle, because
This isn't who you are
Or who you want to be.
You struggle to punish. You struggle to kill.
You struggle to hit the button when it's time.
You do not have the constitution of a bear,
Or the killer instinct of a tiger in its prime;
        What hopeless tenets embank this sparking soul?

Hope!!—and a little bit of, well, let's read a book?

Years from now, you will put on a different outfit,
You will mildly assume your role of savior
On a different planet, one from which
Your famous father has disappeared.
You will do it as if it were all a joke—a comic look—
Which it is, of course. One time, standing on the beach
Near the old Turtle Hermit's house,
Watching the dance and play of the waves
In their eternal rearrangements
You realized how quiet things had become,
So peaceful, bland, and perfect.
You looked up at the sky, the stars,
The distant image of your father in those constellations;
You wished when he returned that he would be
A different person, full of meek patience.

THE CLOWN

he climbs out of the car but
he can't seem to control his body—

he shakes uncontrollably,
his face, beneath the makeup contorts,
that, strange world of an audience

moves circularly in a dizzy
broken cascade of clowned up feeling

circus lights and
a big Bozo moment: *Welcome*
while the little car shrinks in the dizzy stance

smaller than small
Christmas special on the cable
winter night, cereal-bowl-
yellow refrigerator tucked
between his knees

(its sound like: *aaauuueeerrrr*)

his feet like lamps
the dead can see upon
his mouth smeared up
he misses facial expressions
a tiny desk calendar
or a green desk lamp
a locked green drawer and
a replacement key;

ADAM NEIKIRK

his shiny gloved hand
on the wheel of the car
with a bunch of his friends
crammed in the back

god, those were the days

THE GOD OF GAMES

The God of Anger
Howled at me today.

He winked his huge Malthusian eye
And his huge Balduvian eye.

He said "I don't care
What wings impress
Or what retires
To the gleam of instress
I'm tired
Of being second best"

Then the God of Games
Had a field day
At first,
Throwing arrows
Over his shoulder

Where one disused
Another was broken
Lost

When one was used
Another was left
To rot

The God of Death

The God of Sorrow

Ate bone marrow
And tried to call his mother

The God of Jealousy
Was a lousy lover

The God of Too-easy
Was also a lousy lover

The God of Acting Busy
But really having nothing better on
Cradled his phone
Between his head and shoulder

They say from the black night of the phone
A thousand stars fell out

Now we are here together
Two maggots in a war embrace
You say, Is that the leather
On the sole of the shoe
Of the Business God?

I say it is the leather
On the mask of the face
Of the God Who Listens

When rain falls in the garden
And the cat paces by the auburn railing
I make fun of you
For things you cannot change

THE HEADSMAN'S AXE

Tired of life's disappointments, he felt
The weight of the axe in the heft of his hand:
Trying it out like an experiment,
Circling the bannered rogue
Held in chains beneath the gallows

"You can never love her enough," he says,

The chain and veil uncover his face;

"You can never love enough," he says,

Thinking of a person who had once lived here.
Her name was Sheryl, and she lived
In a constant sitting position: oft have I seen
Her sitting on the bed in the late night,
A cogerel in her heart, like a painful ember,
She toils over, or at least nourishes
Like a lost man frets over his low and rude-built fire,
Touching the pain unseen in her arms,
Feeling the echo of trauma in her downcast eyes,
Growing subtly larger and larger in the regard
Of the demonic gods, which watch her from afar;

"You can never do enough," he pants,
Readying his huge and bearded axe,
And ready to scream at the sky from inside
That tattered, black zeyd-cloth hood,
"Though you are but mortal, and lone,
Though you, yourself, are but a meager sneakthief,

Who have never loved anyone, and hath spent
Your days in gathering coin that were not yours,"
He is gritting his teeth, and one by one,
Around them, the little houses, what are left
Of these sea-cottages, with their poor and dutiful tenants,
Awaken softly, in the dawn-smoke, and come
Out of their houses, to see the execution.

He raises the axe above his head. No one
Will be guillotined today: instead,
He will split this rogue in half with the sheer weight
Of the dropping blade, which by a rock's degree
Hath been perfected in the chill of the night.
Little things flit behind the doomed man's eyes:
The taste of an Easter chick,
The sound of wind in the gimlet of the pine trees,
The touch of the floor, when on first waking up,
One stirs from sleep, and preaches to confirm
The true solidity of the world.
The taste of beer, sometimes,
When a score were good,
Or the loving handmaid, or the tempting fruit,
Or any number of possible diversions.

THE IDEA OF WRITING

puts me in a reflective mood, or perhaps,
waking in a reflective mood (before dawn,
while you are sleeping, reflecting on
the fact that I am here in this flat
and here on earth for another day)
makes me think that I should try
to turn my criss-crossed thoughts into something slightly monetizable,
something for which I might win an award
if I can only apply myself and be clever enough

so I get up to go to my computer to write
sometimes holding a line or two in my mind as long as I can
although often these lines do not make any sense
and I begin to dwell on the fact that they don't really make sense
before I have even reached my computer
while I am still in the kitchen making coffee
in the small French press you got me for my birthday
my 36th birthday

soon I have forgotten whatever the line was
it's always something with five metric feet though
there was a period in my life where I wrote exclusively
in lines that have five metric feet for several years
now I can do it automatically, conceiving of whole lines
that are metrically correct but, again, don't make sense

the only way to resist it, in fact, is to do what I am doing now
writing a narrative about my problem—yes, I think it is a problem
I've tried to read more about 'automatic writing' it's a mystical act
apparently and it was done by W.B. Yeats and his wife
and lately I have been reading a book about ufology
and I wonder if my thoughts are automated because they want me
to say something on their behalf, you know
some message that can only be heard in five-foot lines

as soon as I stop and think about writing a line of verse
it will come in like something unbidden, some old-sounding thing
filled with old-sounding words and get me rejected
from the poetry journals, from all of them simultaneously
(I know this because I do simultaneous submissions)

yet at the same time, I am aware
that there are some people who wouldn't consider what
I am doing now poetry at all, and I am inclined
to agree with them, although this still doesn't help me
what I would like to do is find a way
to do this and to do it with the passion and grace
that seem to be activated in my heart by pentameter lines
even though they are apparently rogue thoughts and don't cooperate
with the rest of my life or even want my life as their subject

yet as far as I know—and this is something
I really feel that someone should investigate, someone
besides me, that is, to the extent that I am investigating now
and investigating it in other forms of writing that aren't
poetry or whatever this is—the two simply don't go together;
the focus of the lines, while blurry and vague
(because, in a way, they are necessarily activated
by a kind of ideal language describing ideal activities)
is always something far off, without specificity
while my life, always sitting right in front of my face
is so specific that verse cannot capture it
and the best way to show these two relationships
would be to think about them *abstractly* and then
we'd be off to the races with that one wouldn't we

and if I cut all this out (edited it or simply
didn't countenance it in the first place)
and simply sat down and started to compose verse

Taking my life as with a giant's hand
She does not feel my body in its clothes,
Raising me in her huge, untutored palm
I want to tumble naked from the air
'I' want to fall through clouds and cloudy shifts
Down to a field where I will be obscured
And she can have the outfit I was wearing
And leave me to explore the dew-fresh grass

now in my little green poetry world or whatever it is
I am naked, roaming through the grass
while the sound of the giant's dissipating feet

can be heard in the night like peals of thunder

THE IMAGINATION

I saw it looking at me
In the early morning

A black shape
On the other side
Of a doorway

Its head barely visible
Behind the clouds of sleep
It barely needed
The assistance of its eyes

A pitch-black human figure
Trying to see into my bedroom

Some of you might be thinking
This is the part where he sits on your chest

In your mind, his weight
Has already been applied

Others may shudder
Because they do not know his thoughts—
Good or evil?
Nice, or gross?

In your mind, his weight
Has already been appled

Perhaps cutting him asunder, or in twain
Like a piece of fruit would reveal

ADAM NEIKIRK

An essential corelessness,
An it-ness, after all

No pain, no pleasure
No brain

And the two halves beginning
To form themselves into wholes

What would you propose we do now,
Huh, Einstein?

One half just turned into Einstein

Now Einstein and the black man
Are standing on either side
Of my doorway

Trying to see
Into my bedroom

THERE'S NO PLACE

Like home, I murmur
Throwing the whole casserole into the trash
That's what this is, he thinks
A failed Thanksgiving experiment

Not content
To run his mouth on a message board
Or post his thoughts into oblivion
He builds, now here, a half of a campfire,
Now here a meagre tent, pea-green cloth
Now here, he drags a fallen log to make his seat
And sate among the half of a fairy circle
Cooling his heels in wonderland

Scuppering me for my supper and I rude
I once closed my eyes and had, for a moment
A black and white vision of the American south
Perfectly poor, perfectly preserved
In my mind like the start of a very old film

I mean an old movie
Diverting myself from the truth
How, after enough time has passed
All you notice is what doesn't seem contemporary
The message is lost, and we
Cannot hear the birdman making convincing squarks
In a language that is not his own

God help me, he squarks

ADAM NEIKIRK

Applying a huge, fake beak to his own face
With a snappy rubber band

THOU'RT STILL COOL

If metered poetry's an old man's game,
It hardly merits that an idle king
Is already older and lamer than I am;
It need not carry on without a spring
Or lack of loading up a different chime;
It can be something vital to our time.

Sometimes the interest's only in the thing
That you have said in the sequestered line
That you are reading; O you have forgot
The argument (and it could use explaining),
But reading's difficult and it's a lot
To take in all at once; yet you're still trying

To grasp at hues of sense when they appear
Like watching gardens when the sun has glimpsed
Above the gate of shadow, and the fear
Of it is pushing fire through the fence.

O golden reason, tell me the good news:
The seeds have last the night, and now, in earth
They're shut up listening for the knocking light
Striking hard upon the colder dark.

TITLE

It's a mystery to me, how, after writing two books
You managed to wrangle the world into an accord
Full of well-meaning, if mistaken looks
I think it was because the people reading your work
Somehow had a different expectation, that you
Would somehow revise them or return
The height of verse to its former purview
These are just my established thoughts
On the non-possibility of knowing the truth

Dwelling on that boundary-line of mystery
With the not-so-distant past occupying
The other side, its look and general description
Waiting for the familiar rhythm and the sound
Of one's long line whispering to the other,
Running in bare feet across the promised ground
As if to go from one place to another,
Waiting for the smile and the nod to 'kick in'
As if this actually had something to do with running

Using poetry merely to contemplate your life,
Bad poetry, that deliberately refuses access
Either through felicitous description of 'real life'
Or through the realizing power of better verse,
Thinking on the surface of the jumbled lines
Like skating on uneven ground with bladeless boots,
One waits for the real thing to appear in time,
One waits for the part that seems especially planned,
When everything seems to be in cahoots

TO BE READ AS IF ...

On his knees in the church babbling with a hurdling voice he said

I think you wake up every day convinced
I do not love you

Please God
Love me today

When I see your face
Emerging from the darkened room at first
Light and we remember we have chosen
To bear the weight of life together I

Feel like a "God ray"
Through the looking glass in its respect of blue—
Or like a moveless statue, made of stone,
The smooth white marble face, the half-interested aspect
—

Part of me stops by on a Sunday afternoon,
Pastorally encouraging you to chit and chat,
Eating some of your food, drinking some wine,
Occasionally reminding you of infinite love;

On another hand, the rogue in me has died:
He was split in two,
And as you look over your shoulder
At the things that haunt you

Please God
Let me love her today

I step into this mind palace, this little place
Of desperate prayer, ready to babble and drool
And live on my knees, in abject subjugation
If that is what it takes to be [made] good.

In a short dream, two people dressed in white
With pale skin like the flour of the bread
Hath coated them, together meet beside
A shallow pool, set by itself inside
The uncertain embrace of a woodland.
There they meet beneath
The happy shadows of pine trees,
Embracing, kissing, edging themselves to ward
The Idea of Passion, while the moon froths in the pondlight;
The tall pines, dark, forbidding, like tall stone,
Like wooden struts, like foundational, load-bearing walls,
Hang over them like curtains of ash and lace,
And hide them in the dark, the near, close dark
Like that of so many nights that we have enjoyed.

VAST COMPASS

A page which says
Last Will and Testament of Harry R. Stoneback
Rests gently on the table, fresh arrived
From across the ocean, from where I've just returned.

I didn't visit your house, where it stands empty,
Or go to your grave, where, probably the choked voices
Can still be heard. I wasn't there when you died.

It is four
Or five pages only,
Paragraphs close, stricken-looking,
A little oddly with an antique speech,
Made miserable—

"A resident
Of / and domiciled at /"

Somehow noncommittal, even casual,
Against the backdrop of your learning.

"28 Maple Avenue, Highland, Town of Lloyd,
County of Ulster, and State of New York"

That's all, a place we found on Google Maps,
A barrage of secretive trees cover over
Every bit of the house, excepting its tall tower.
I wanted to take your hand and lead you down

Through the yard, from the wrap-around porch,

From out of the door, with its turn-key bell ringer,
Over the small fish-pond, with its bridge for sitting and feeding,
Although that pond has been dry for many years,

And over the wall at the back of the grass, piled with white stone,
Down into the woods and leaves, still dark and forbidding,
Where, maybe someday,
Someone would walk, stepping carefully,
Crying over your bones;

Or up through the doors,
And over the dusty hallway,
With its basically useless piano you still played,

Up the broad staircase, to the room where you slept,
Often 'til noon, in a shirt the color of summer,
Or beyond it, to the places where we laid
Counting the sounds of crickets, reading the spines of *Gnomes*?

Into the third floor, a fantasy for most people nowadays,
Filled with its fifty thousand volumes of university material,
An alchemist's quarters if you had the "quarters" for it—

The huge red feather bed with nothing in it—

WAITING ROOM OF THE DAMNED

Let it slam down deep, and let it be
A soft reminder to regard yourself
As prone the minute you feel that you have
Arrived home. The longer you put it off,
The more it feels like something that ought
To have happened already; because of that, it seems
Ineluctably real; waking to the rise in the morning
At 3 a.m., the riot in the blood,
A curse on you and all you might've been,
Sugare, sucre, which one had imbibed,
At midnight with the sanctity of day,
And pushes both the soothing thought of rest,
And the rousing thought of action far away.
Get in line, fall in, and you will see
What passes for action on a day like this.
This office, with its ethereal mist,
An electably feminine head nurse, who is dead,
And yet in death, having found her cosmic purpose,
Tracing her muted finger on a list,
She has found more purchase than the pinkest flesh.

You stood beneath the treeline at the school,
You also sought, sometimes, by the black fence
Which like a rusted hedgerow in itself
Stood on the far side of the rugby field
To escape through a tear in the metal of the fence
Which seems now as if someone put it there

Almost in defense—to flee the world
That they could not go missing—or barring that,
To leave with such abandon
That time itself would stop. Then go
Into that leafy wilderness, ill-concealed by that grey fence,
The green world ill-concealed by rust and dust
Which drifted in in droves from the grass-shorn track,
And with a kind of flower in the heart,
A four-piece, or a cotton bud, or clover,
Go on unlooking, neither looking, nor glancing back.

YOUR VALLEY LIFE IS A FANTASY LIFE

What did you think? That there were mountains, burrows,
Mines replete with garnished goods, worm-tunnels,
Kingstombs, and bamboo forests
Where rather than growing in silence, clouds emit
From the edges of trees, flung like whimsical feelings
Filled, as are all worthwhile feelings, with rain?

ABOUT THE AUTHOR

Adam Neikirk

Adam Neikirk is a scholar and poet with research interests in Romanticism, metrical poetry, and philosophy of literature. In 2023, he received his PhD in Creative Writing from the University of Essex with a creative thesis about the philosopher and poet Samuel Taylor Coleridge. Adam has also published two previous books of poetry: Songs for the Dead (2016), on which this book is based, and Itchy (2022), published by Muscaliet Press. His critical writings have appeared in the Coleridge Bulletin and Forum journal. He currently lives in the United States with his wife.

You can find Adam on Twitter/X @tweets4thedead.

BOOKS BY THIS AUTHOR

Songs For The Dead (2016)

Itchy (2022)

Made in the USA
Middletown, DE
08 April 2024